A **Century of Prayer**
for Christian Unity

A **Century of Prayer**
for Christian Unity

Edited by

Catherine E. Clifford

William B. Eerdmans Publishing Company
Grand Rapids, Michigan / Cambridge, U.K.

Published 2009 by
Wm. B. Eerdmans Publishing Co.
2140 Oak Industrial Drive N.E., Grand Rapids, Michigan 49505 /
P.O. Box 163, Cambridge CB3 9PU U.K.

Printed in the United States of America

14 13 12 11 10 09   7 6 5 4 3 2 1

ISBN 978-0-8028-6366-9

www.eerdmans.com

Table of Contents

Abbreviations

APUC	Association for the Promotion of the Unity of Christendom
ARCIC	Anglican-Roman Catholic International Commission
DV	*Dei Verbum* (Vatican II's Dogmatic Constitution on Divine Revelation)
LG	*Lumen Gentium* (Vatican II's Dogmatic Constitution on the Church)
NMI	*Novo Millennio Inuente* (Pope John Paul II's Apostolic letter at the close of the Great Jubilee Year 2000)
UR	*Unitatis Redintegratio* (Vatican II's Decree on Ecumenism)
UUS	*Ut Unum Sint* (Pope John Paul II's encyclical on Commitment to Ecumenism)
YMCA	Young Men's Christian Association
YWCA	Young Women's Christian Association

What would the ecumenical movement become without the personal or communal prayer that "they may all be one; even as you, Father, are in me, and I in you" (John 17: 21)? Where would we find the "extra impetus" of faith, hope and charity, of which our search for unity has a special need today? Our desire for unity must not be limited to isolated occasions; it must become an integral part of our whole prayer life. (…)

Let us thank God for the great prayer movement which for 100 years has accompanied and sustained believers in Christ in their quest for unity. The ship of ecumenism would never have put out to sea had she not been lifted by this broad current of prayer and wafted by the breath of the Holy Spirit.

Pope Benedict XVI
Homily for Vespers on the Feast of the Conversion of St. Paul
for the Conclusion of the Week of Prayer for Christian Unity
Basilica of Saint Paul Outside the Walls
25 January 2008

Introduction

Prayer: The Soul of Ecumenical Renewal

CATHERINE E. CLIFFORD

God has no need of our prayer. Whether by praise and thanksgiving or supplication and intercession, we can hardly expect to add anything to the God that theologians have described as a perfect, immutable, and infinite Supreme Being, or that the transcendent being at the source of all creation might ever be changed through our feeble human efforts at persuasion. The secret of prayer is not that we can hope to influence the utterly transcendent one, but that prayer changes *us*. The practice of prayer opens us to the transforming activity of the Holy Spirit. The discipline of prayer teaches us to be attentive and responsive to the ways and the desires of God in our lives. It opens our hearts to receive the gift of transforming love. Prayer has often been called a school of the heart. It is a school of love, of communion. Saint Paul reminds us that our hope lies not in the expectation of changing God, but in the fact that "the love of God has been poured into our hearts through the Holy Spirit that has been given to us" (Romans 5:5). Through the incarnation of God's Word in Christ, God's love has been revealed to us in a most personal and intimate way and has shone on the face of Jesus. Prayer is therefore the expression of a personal relationship with God as we respond to the stirring of the Spirit who prays in us, through Christ, to the Father.

Another word for that love of God is communion, the relationship shared by the divine Trinity of persons and the overflowing of their inner life for us. The Christian tradition has spoken in various ways about this mystery as our participation in the divine life of the Trinity or as the indwelling of God's Spirit in our hearts. The mystery of our communion with God is not a private affair to be enjoyed in an individualistic way. The word church, from the Greek *ecclesia* in the New Testament, refers to a people who have been called apart and gathered together by God. In the economy of Christian salvation God does not save us as individuals but as members of this people, this community we call the church. Entering fully into a relationship of communion with God implies that our relationships with others are also changed. It implies the gift and the responsibility of living together with others in communion, this communion that we call the church.

Further, the church is not an end in itself. It has a vocation in the world to collaborate in bringing about God's desire for unity and concord among all peoples and harmony in all of creation. Ecclesial unity is at the service of the mission of the church. Unity, therefore, belongs to the very essence of the church of God. Disunity reflects our inability, due to human weakness and sin, to welcome the Spirit's gift and let the love of God that now dwells in our hearts be poured out for others. If unity is the work of God's Spirit, then the healing of division can only come about when we make room for the Spirit through the practice of prayer.

"Pray without ceasing" (1 Thessalonians 5:17) is the theme for the annual celebration of the Week of Prayer for Christian Unity in this year, 2008, which marks the one hundredth anniversary of its observance. Paul exhorts the members of the young church at Thessalonica to be patient and long-suffering with one another and to "rejoice always" in the presence of God which has gathered them together. Prayer without ceasing might be seen as a practical expression of this constant joy. It means living always in the presence of God, cultivating a permanent awareness of God who is the source of all creation and whose love is present in every moment of our personal and communal journey, even in those moments when are least aware of it. This same grace of God is the source of the life of the church and makes of it more than a purely human community. It is a grace-filled communion where, though we might live in a constant tension between human sinfulness and Spirit blessed holiness, sin and division can never have the last word. When we practice the discipline of prayer without ceasing, our attention is focused not on the impossibility of human limitations, but on the God-given gifts of transforming grace.

Prayer for unity has been one of the characteristic features of Christian prayer from the earliest times. The *Didache*, one of the earliest texts that give us a window into the prayer life of early Christians, contains this invocation recited at the celebration of the Lord's Supper: "As this broken bread was scattered upon the mountains, but was brought together and became one, so let thy Church be gathered together from the ends of the earth into thy Kingdom" (9:4).[1] This prayer reflects a profound awareness on the part of the early Christian community of having been called together, in all their diversity, into one by God. The history of the church is marked by a constant struggle to remain faithful to this calling, and at times by sad and dramatic failures to do so. Some of these tensions are inherent in holding the rich diversity of Christian theological, liturgical, and spiritual traditions in balance. Others are a reflection of sin and alienation. So Christians have always prayed for the unity of the church, one of the four essential notes that we refer to in the Nicene Creed. The way in which we relate to each other is a matter of fidelity to our vocation as the community gathered together by the love of God. As the Dogmatic Constitution of the Church (*Lumen Gentium*) describes it, in Christ we are called to be "like a sacrament or as a sign and instrument both of a very closely knit union with God and of the unity of the whole human race" (*LG* 1).

In the past century, Christians have been engaged more intentionally in the effort to work and pray for the reconciliation of the divided churches. With the expansion of horizons brought about by increased possibilities for communication and travel and the accompanying missionary élan of the churches in the nineteenth century came the awareness that division contradicts the message of the gospel, undermines the church's mission, and saps vital energies from the ecclesial body that could be put to use in common witness and service to the world. Christians began to organize themselves and reevaluate their understanding of mission and common witness, to find new ways to act together in service of the human community, and to consider the doctrinal questions that had been the basis of their separation. This gave rise to organizations such as the International Missionary Council (Edinburgh, 1910), Life and Work (Stockholm, 1925), and Faith in Order (Lausanne, 1927), which were later integrated to form the World Council of Churches (1948).

The Catholic Church entered fully into this multidimensional ecumenical movement when Pope John XXIII called the bishops of the church together for the Second Vatican Council (1962-1965), which had as its purpose was the restoration of Christian unity, and the related goal of *aggiornamento*, the updating and renewal of the Catholic Church. John XXIII understood ecclesial renewal and reform, undertaken in fidelity to the gospel, as the essential path toward the restoration of unity. In the past forty years extensive progress has been achieved through formal bilateral and multilateral theological dialogues to overcome many the church dividing issues. Many Christians now recognize one another's baptism and can now easily marry members of other Christian churches. These are things that many take for granted today, but which were not a given just a few short decades ago. Historic agreements have been signed on christological doctrine between the Catholic Church and several Oriental Orthodox Churches, and on the central debate of the Protestant Reformation, the doctrine of justification by faith, between the Catholic Church and the Lutheran World Federation. Lutherans and Anglicans have entered into full communion in Europe and North America, and many Lutheran and Reformed Churches have concluded similar agreements.

Surely none of these significant steps could have been achieved if hearts had not been changed and minds had not been opened through the practice of prayer in common. We should not underestimate the formative power of prayer in preparing us as individuals and as churches to begin to recognize the presence and action of God's Spirit in the theology and life of one another's Christian traditions. How else could we have progressed from considering other Christians as simply mistaken, to the discovery that "various theological formulations are often to be considered as complementary rather than conflicting" (UR 17)? Indeed, after a century of prayer for Christian unity we can say with confidence that Christians have moved "from antagonism and conflict to a situation where each party recognizes the other as a partner."[2]

To be effective, the practice of prayer for Christian unity, which can be part of each church's life of prayer separately, but which also includes a commitment to prayer in common with other Christians, must become a constant feature of ecclesial life and should not be limited to annual gatherings during the Week of Prayer for Christian Unity. Cardinal Walter Kasper has recently recognized the necessity of making the culture of common prayer and spirituality a high priority for the future progress of the ecumenical movement by issuing a very practical *Handbook of Spiritual Ecumenism.*[3] The question of spiritual ecumenism, and more specifically of common prayer for the reconciliation and visible unity of the Christian churches, is a matter of concern for every baptized Christian. At stake is the faithfulness of Christians to their calling in the world. The pioneers of prayer for unity understood this well. Their insight was received in the teaching of the Decree on Ecumenism (*Unitatis Redintegratio*) at Vatican II, and was reiterated by Pope John Paul II in his historic encyclical on commitment to ecumenism, *Ut Unum Sint*, when he wrote: "prayer is to be the 'soul' of ecumenical renewal and of the yearning for unity; it is the basis and support for everything the Council defines as 'dialogue.'"[4] Common prayer is the foundation for every other expression of ecumenical life.

One Hundred Years of Prayer for Christian Unity

This book is intended to mark the centenary celebration of the Week of Prayer for Christian Unity as well as the influence of the founders of the religious community of the Franciscan Friars and Sisters of the Atonement, Father Paul Wattson and Sister Lurana White, in its establishment. Lurana White began a common life with two companions in Graymoor, New York in December of 1898.[5] The following spring they were joined there by Paul Wattson. Together Wattson and White founded the Franciscan Society of the Atonement.[6] Their small community evolved initially within the American Episcopal Church. Wattson and White were deeply influenced by movements within Anglicanism during this period that fervently hoped for reconciliation with the Church of Rome. Their initiative can be seen against the background of other movements of prayer for unity begun earlier in the nineteenth century among Evangelicals and Anglicans. Paul Wattson,[7] together with his friend Spencer Jones in England, established the Octave of Prayer for Christian Unity in 1908. The following year the friars and sisters were officially received into the Roman Catholic Church. Pope Pius X officially recognized the Octave of Prayer in 1916, and soon after Pope Benedict XV extended its observance throughout the Catholic Church. The commitment to work and pray for Christian unity remains at the heart of the ministry of the Franciscan Friars and Sisters of the Atonement today.

Wattson's broad vision for the reestablishment of Christian unity was not fully realized in the earliest form of the Octave of Prayer. For Wattson, unity did not imply the disappearance or absorption of other Christian churches into a uniform body identified with the Church of Rome. He looked forward to a form of corporate reunion that would maintain the rich diversity of Christian traditions. The Octave, however, focused initially on the idea of the return of other Christians to the fold of Roman Catholicism, a focus symbolized in the dates chosen for its observance, from January 18 (then the Feast of the Chair of Peter) to January 25 (the Feast of the Conversion of St. Paul in the liturgical calendar of the day). It took the insight of Father Paul Couturier to develop a form of prayer which was more explicitly Christ centered and opened the way for the participation of all Christians in a common intercession for the unity that Christ desires in a "universal" Week of Prayer. This was very much in line with Wattson's understanding of the connection between ecclesial communion and a common engagement to carry on the mission of Christ.

Both of these pioneers understood ecclesial communion to be a gift of the Spirit. Both understood that Christians could not begin to be reconciled amongst themselves without opening themselves to receive that grace through prayer. Both placed the prayer of Christ at the center of their vision of the annual celebration of the Week of Prayer. For Wattson, it was impossible to consider that Jesus' prayer to the Father for his disciples, "that they may all be one ... so that the world may believe" (John 17:21), would be left unanswered by God. Couturier was moved by the conviction that Christians must put on the very mind of Christ and make his prayer their own if they were to realize his will for the church and their calling in the world. Praying for the unity that Christ desires is a matter of bringing the will of Christians in tune with the will of Christ. Since the time of the Second Vatican Council the World Council of Church's Commission on Faith and Order and the Vatican's Pontifical Council for the Promotion of Christian Unity have collaborated in the preparation and the promotion of the Week of Prayer for Christian Unity around the world.

About the Essays in this Volume

This book is a celebration of the history of the Week of Prayer for Christian Unity and a wonderful resource for understanding the theology and practice of common prayer for the reconciliation of the churches. The contributors to this volume represent a cross section of perspectives both denominationally and in light of their lived experience of Christian spirituality and prayer. They provide us with important insights into the history, theology, and spirituality of the Week of Prayer in particular, and of ecumenical prayer in general.

Cardinal Walter Kasper, reflects on the spirituality implied in the observance of the Week of Prayer on the occasion of the centenary of its observance. His remarks are taken from his address to a gathering at the Centro Pro Unione in Rome for the conferral of the Paul Wattson Christian Unity Award by the Franciscan Friars and Sisters of the Atonement on the Pontifical Council for Christian Unity and the Faith and Order Commission of the World Council of Churches. These two agencies have worked collaboratively in promoting the observance of the Week of Prayer since the time of the Second Vatican Council. As we stand on the threshold of what he views as a new phase in the ecumenical life of the church, Kasper invites all Christians to go deeper into the spirituality which gave rise to the modern ecumenical movement. He proposes a number of criteria for discerning the authenticity of our ecumenical engagement and for grounding a true spiritual ecumenism that must be at the heart of any and all activity directed toward the reconciliation of the churches.

In an essay that explores the observance of the Week of Prayer for Christian Unity through the twentieth century, James Puglisi, the Minister General of the Friars of the Atonement, considers the theology of Christian prayer that underlies the practice of intercession for the unity of the church and praise for the communion that we already share. He documents the significant change of mindset that occurred in the observance of the Week of Prayer and that enabled a shift from a praying "for the return to the Mother Church or for unity within one's own church" to the practice of common prayer focused on the common mission of Christians in the world. After an examination of the themes of the Week of Prayer in the four decades since the Second Vatican Council, Puglisi considers the challenge of the present context and insists on the need to make prayer for Christian unity much more than an annual observance, but a "daily exercise."

Charles Sherlock presents a comprehensive overview of the Anglican tradition of prayer, especially through the lens of Anglican liturgical practice. It is interesting to observe how the Church of England gave primacy of place to the idea of unity within its own ecclesial family, easily identified in various historical circumstances with unity within the realm. The end of a unified experience of Christendom coincides with a growing consciousness, through the experience of colonization and the concomitant expansion of Christian mission (both within the Anglican Communion and in other Christian churches), of becoming a world church with new challenges to maintaining unity. This new awareness is reflected in the calls of the Lambeth Conferences of the Anglican Communion to observe "a season of prayer for the unity of Christendom" in the late nineteenth century. The initiative of Paul Wattson and Spencer Jones to establish the Octave of Prayer in 1908 can be seen as a further development of this practice within the Anglican tradition. A close examination of Paul Couturier reveals that he, too, was deeply inspired by a close bond of friendship with Anglicanism.[8] Sherlock concludes by reflecting on how the revision of Anglican prayer books under the influence of the very ecumenical movement of liturgical renewal in the 1970s and 80s marks an end to the colonial models of unity that had marked the spirit of many Anglican prayers. New ecumenical prayers and cycles of prayer have made prayer for the reconciliation of Christians a more integral part of the Anglican liturgical culture.

We are privileged to include in this volume the personal testimony of George Tavard who was part of the team of experts who worked with the Secretariat for the Promotion of Christian Unity to draft the section of the Decree on Ecumenism devoted to spiritual ecumenism during the Second Vatican Council. Father Tavard died very soon after having submitted the manuscript for this chapter, and his loss touches all who knew him. His work stands as a significant historical witness to the moment when the Catholic Church, no doubt as one of the fruits of a half century of prayer, embraced the spirituality implied in the observance of the Week of Prayer. The council encourages us to take advantage of every opportunity to join other Christians in prayer, for prayer leads to "conversion of heart and holiness of life" (UR 8). Moreover, the Decree on Ecumenism recognizes that growth toward spiritual maturity and holiness is intimately linked to the renewal of the life of the whole church. This renewal, to be characterized by a spirit of humility and repentance, is the path to becoming church more fully, and is the only path which the council envisions for the restoration of unity. The council declares that spiritual ecumenism is to be understood as the heart of the ecumenical movement. Tavard offers a first-hand account of the elaboration of the texts relating to these themes.

Closely related to the rise of the ecumenical movement – which is linked on so many levels to a return to the common heritage of the Christian tradition in the biblical and patristic sources – is the reappearance of monastic and religious communities within Anglican and Protestant churches. Sister Minke de Vries reflects on the example of the Community of Grandchamp, a community born within the Swiss Reformed tradition. Today women from a variety of Protestant churches share the monastic way of life at Grandchamp following the Rule of Taizé and praying daily for the unity of the churches. Sister Minke details the exchanges of the founders of the community with Paul Couturier and the way in which the spirit that informs the Week of Prayer continues to inform the spirituality of the community today. The prophetic witness of this and other ecumenical communities is a source of inspiration and an important resource for the churches as they seek to live in closer communion with one another.

Some readers might consider the witness of the Baptist tradition to be an unlikely voice to include in a collection of essays dedicated to the Week of Prayer for Christian Unity. Steven R. Harmon readily acknowledges that the reputation of Baptists as being largely averse to involvement in the ecumenical movement is not entirely undeserved. He considers how Baptist eschatologies might be responsible in part for keeping many Baptists at arm's length from engaging in the search for visible ecclesial unity. Where overemphasis on realized eschatology favors negative attitudes toward other churches, undue stress on the realization of God's plan in the future can lead to a neglect of the necessity for renewal of one's own church in the present.

Harmon proposes that the eschatology implied in the act of praying for Christian unity is one that is very much in harmony with a Baptist vision of the church's responsibility to embody the eschatological future in the concrete historical reality of the church in this moment of history. The spirituality of the Week of Prayer holds in tension and balance the already and not-yet of the realization of the church's calling in the world. His reflection is a timely invitation to many in the Free Church and Evangelical streams of Christian tradition to find a home within the spirit of the Week of Prayer, a spirit that summons all Christ's disciples to put on the heart and mind of their master. Harmon argues that this spirituality extends beyond an idea of unity that envisions the goal as communion among Christian individuals in a movement of spiritual renewal. Spiritual ecumenism yes, but not spiritualized ecumenism! The bonds of Christian unity will be expressed concretely and visibly in through the mutual recognition of baptism and in one eucharistic fellowship.

The Week of Prayer in the Present Context of the Churches

A number of contributors comment on the challenge of the present ecumenical context. If we are not in a full blown "winter" of the ecumenical movement, we have nonetheless been through a real "cooling off" period in the past decade of interchurch relations. The effervescence of renewing relationships of friendship and trust and the initial excitement of discovering the unity we share on many issues that were once considered to be church dividing has given way to experiences of frustration, impatience, lassitude, and apathy. Attitudes of mutual suspicion persist on many levels. Many today are openly skeptical about the possibility of visible church unity and consider the goals of the ecumenical movement as unrealistic and unworthy of the time and effort.

These sentiments are compounded by the growing complexity of Christianity. In the past century we witnessed the rapid and unprecedented expansion of Evangelical and Pentecostal movements which many scholars now call the "third wave" of Christianity. The old established churches, namely the Orthodox Churches of the East, and the Catholic, Anglican, and classical Protestant churches with roots in the sixteenth century Reformation, now struggle to come to terms with being "disestablished" as the synthesis of Christendom comes to a close, especially in the West. Their place in society now uncertain, they must renegotiate their stance in the world. As one friend has put it, today the "main line" churches are being side lined! Preoccupied with declining levels of participation and the challenge of finding a credible voice in a secular and religiously pluralistic world, many Christian churches are more interested today in shoring up a sense of their own denominational identity than in building relationships with other Christian groups. Increasing polarization within denominational communities reinforces the desire for a stronger sense of identity and the need to focus more on the unity of one's own church than on unity with others. Ecumenism and ecumenical prayer are not a high priority on the agenda for many church leaders.

In light of recent international conflicts and rising rates of immigration to the West by men and women of other religious traditions, the question of religious pluralism and of interreligious dialogue often captures the imagination more readily today than matters of unity among the Christian churches. At moments of national significance it has now become fashionable, and indeed it is right, to have leaders of the great world religions gather together in solidarity and prayer. Such celebrations are a welcome development in a religiously pluralistic context. The Christian community no longer enjoys hegemony in the public and civic life of Western societies. Nonetheless, these developments should not distract us from the irreplaceable resource represented by the common experience of Christians gathered together in prayer and growing together in unity. If Christians are to enter fully into dialogue with members of non-Christian religious traditions, our efforts will only be credible when we can speak with one voice and witness to our common faith together. In truth, the pressing need for harmony among the great religions in the context of the world community should heighten our sense of the urgent need for Christians to be reconciled, and of the necessity of strengthening our commitment to common prayer.

The Gospel of Luke includes an account of the encounter between Jesus and several disciples on the shore of Lake Gennesaret. The disciples had been fishing all night long and had caught nothing. They were dispirited when Jesus got into one of their boats and asked them to put their nets out into the deep water (Luke 5:1-4). Perhaps after a century of celebrating the Week of Prayer for Christian Unity we too are wondering whether our efforts have been for naught. What's the use? Why go on? Though we might be tempted at times to say that unity is still far off and hardly worth hoping for lest we be disappointed, we cannot ignore the tremendous steps that have been taken toward the reconciliation of the churches in the past one hundred years. Now after a century of prayer we are invited to go deeper, to sound the depths of our common faith together in prayer, to draw from the unique source of our communion in the life of the divine Trinity. Let us take heart and sing with praise and rejoicing without ceasing to the God who calls us together. Let us not shy away from the high calling that is ours as members of Christ's body. The apostles were not disappointed and brought in their nets full to breaking with fish. When Christians go deeper and dare to stand together in prayer before God we shall learn to receive what we are: a visible sign of the outpouring of God's love for the world.

Chapter One

The Week of Prayer for Christian Unity: Origin and Continuing Inspiration of the Ecumenical Movement

CARDINAL WALTER KASPER

The celebration of the Week of Prayer for the unity of all Christians in this year 2008 has its special momentum.* We celebrate this year, so to speak, the one hundredth birthday of this yearly recurring event. At the same time we also celebrate the fortieth anniversary of the joint preparation of the materials for the Week of Prayer by the Commission of Faith and Order of the World Council of Churches together with the Pontifical Council for Promoting Christian Unity. And because all good things come in three, we also commemorate this year the memorable fact that twenty-five years ago, precisely during the Week of Prayer, Pope John Paul II beatified the Trappistine nun Maria Gabriella of Unity, who sacrificed her whole life to meditation and prayer for the realization of Jesus' own prayer "that all may be one."

This threefold anniversary gives me reason to reflect on the history and the binding legacy of the ecumenical movement, especially of the Week of Prayer and of spiritual ecumenism, and to reflect then on what spiritual ecumenism is all about and what its

---

* First given at the Centrio Pro Unione on the occasion of the conferral of the Paul Wattson Christian Unity Award to the Pontifical Council for the Promotion of Christian Unity and the Faith and Order Commission of the World Council of Churches, January 24, 2008.

momentum is, particularly in our ecumenical situation which in many aspects is changing and at the beginning of the twenty-first century is on the threshold of a new phase of its history.

The Origins of the Ecumenical Movement and the Week of Prayer

It is generally acknowledged that the ecumenical movement of the twentieth century started with the World Missionary Conference in Edinburgh in 1910, whose coming hundredth anniversary in two years we are already preparing together. There are strong reasons for this. For Edinburgh was a very important event for different reasons. It was the source of the two main streams leading to the World Council of Churches: "Life and Work," and "Faith and Order." The very legacy of Edinburgh is the indissoluble togetherness of the ecumenical and the missionary commitment of the church. Ecumenism and mission are, so to speak, siblings; both of them make clear and sharp our ecclesial consciousness that the church can never be self-sufficient, but must look beyond itself and transcend itself. In ecumenism the church is challenged to become aware of the scandal of the division so plainly made visible by the existence of other churches and ecclesial communities and to try to achieve reconciliation; in mission the church has to open itself to the world of nations, which are longing for the message of the gospel. Therefore, ecumenism and mission also have an eschatological dimension; they strive towards eschatological *shalom*. So it was not by accident that the two moderators in Edinburgh were also protagonists in the peace movement which started after the catastrophe and devastation of the First World War.

But as important and worthy as it is to commemorate Edinburgh, it is not the only and not the oldest root of twentieth century ecumenism. One hundred years ago the Episcopalian minister Paul Wattson, cofounder of the Society of the friars and sisters of the Atonement in Graymoor (Garrison, New York), introduced an Octave of prayer for the unity of Christians, which was celebrated for the first time from 18 to 25 January 1908. Therefore, the preparation of this year's Week of Prayer can trace its origins to Graymoor. The Superior of the Atonement friars today is the director of the "Centro Pro Unione" here in Rome.

The precedents of the Week of Prayer go back even further to several initiatives and revival movements in the second half of the nineteenth century. They can be found in the Oxford movement, the World Evangelical Alliance, the women's "World Day of Prayer," which despite strong male opposition was initiated by Presbyterian, Methodist, Baptist, Anglican women in the eighties of the nineteenth century, commencing in the United States and Canada and then spreading throughout the whole world. Decisive as well were the youth movements of the YMCA and YWCA, which were present also in Edinburgh. John Mott, Methodist pastor and one of the presidents in Edinburgh, wrote: "The heart of Edinburgh was not in its speeches, but in its periods of prayer."

In a particular way, it is worthy to commemorate the two encyclicals of the Ecumenical Patriarch Joachim III, the first in 1902 to all Orthodox churches and then the encyclical in 1920 in which he invited the churches of all the world to an "Alliance of Churches" similar to the then "Alliance of Nations." In this encyclical the Patriarch not only used the Greek term *koinonia* (communion) already as ultimate goal of the reunification of the churches, but underlined also that for all Christians the unity among all Christians is an object of permanent prayer and supplication.

The Catholic Church did not stand back. Though it joined the ecumenical movement officially only with the Decree On Ecumenism (*Unitatis redintegratio*) of the Second Vatican Council (1962-65), it took part in the prayer for Christian unity from the very beginning. Already in 1895 Pope Leo XIII recommended a Week of Prayer in the week before Pentecost. When the Society of the Atonement became Catholic in a corporate way, Pope Pius X in 1909 gave his official benediction to the Week of Prayer in January. Pope Benedict XV introduced and recommended the Week definitively in the wider Catholic Church. Pope Pius XI promoted the Week of Prayer as well, and Pope Pius XII stated, in his encyclical

Mystici corporis (1943), that he himself would pray for the unity of the church following the example of Christ. It is noteworthy that Pope John XXIII on January 25, 1959, the concluding day of the Week of Prayer, announced the Second Vatican Council, which opened the Catholic Church officially to the ecumenical movement.

But looking back again to the original intention of Paul Wattson we can recognise an important development within the concept of the Week of Prayer. Whereas Paul Wattson understood the goal of unity as the return to the bosom of the Catholic Church, Abbé Paul Couturier from Lyon in France gave a new and, in the proper sense, a very ecumenical impulse to the Week of Prayer in the nineteen thirties. He changed the name from "Church Unity Octave" to "Universal Week of Prayer for the Unity of Christians," thereby propagating a unity of the church, "as Christ wishes and by the means which he desires." His spiritual testament, where he explains his intentions in a very moving and spiritually very profound way, is one of the most inspiring ecumenical texts and therefore still worthwhile reading and meditating on. Paul Couturier became influential for the Groupe des Dombes and for Roger Schutz and the community of Taizé; he was also the inspiration for Maria Gabriella.

To conclude this short historical résumé, we can state that the origins of the Week of Prayer tell us different and very important things:

First, the theme of this year's Week of Prayer "Pray without ceasing!" (1 Thessalonians 5:17) condenses a long history going back more than 100 years, in the final analysis to the Cenacle in Jerusalem. There is from the very beginning a strong spiritual force behind the ecumenical movement. Its very origin and deep motive is Jesus' prayer to his Father on the eve of his passion and death, "that they may all be one ... as you, Father, and I ... are one" (John 17:21-22). Thus the very goal is communion, but a communion which is not a pure human achievement, but a gift and above all a mystery. When, where and how this unity will take place, is not in our hands, but in God's. In Him we can trust.

Second, the ecumenical awareness started more or less independently in different circles and church traditions across confessional and national boundaries. From its very beginning it was largely supported by all church traditions: the Anglican, the Evangelical, the Free Church, the Orthodox and the Catholic. It cannot be understood in any other way than as an impulse and work of the Holy Spirit, who awakened Christians all over the world and in all church traditions, made them aware of the scandal of division and inspired in them the desire for unity.

Third, through Edinburgh and what followed from it, i.e., the movements "Life and Work" and "Faith and Order," the primarily spiritual movement was for the first time able to channel itself as an institutional structure, merging with the missionary commitment and the peace movement and thus reaching not only a worldwide but even more a very world-dimension. For each year when praying for the unity of all Christians we pray also for all the real social and political needs and for peace in the world. Also this last point seems to me a response to the signs of the times. In a century which was one of the most dark and bloody in history, where two world wars cost the lives of millions, where two totalitarian systems and many dictatorships produced countless innocent victims, Christians stood up to overcome their centuries old divisions, giving witness to the fact that despite guilt in the past on all sides, reconciliation is possible. Really, in the last century ecumenism was a light shining in the darkness and a powerful peace movement.

Spiritual Empathy

In the last hundred years, which we commemorate this year, the ecumenical movement has made great progress. More important than individual results and the extensive production of ecumenical documents has been – as Pope John Paul II told us – the rediscovery of brotherhood among the Christians. Undoubtedly, we have not reached the goal of visible unity, we are still divided and sometimes new controversies arise. But what is also important is that a new atmosphere, a new climate, a network of friendship have emerged. The desire for full communion has matured and Christians in many parts of the world and often in the most difficult ones, give common witness not only through their words but through their deeds working for social justice, freedom and peace.

Despite this positive progress, however, situations and moods have also changed. The initial enthusiasm seems to be lost. Some speak even of a crisis, others of an ecumenical winter. I do not like such faint-hearted statements. If it is true that the Holy Spirit initiated the ecumenical movement, then he will bring it also to its goal. So I prefer to speak about a change and a shift in ecumenism. For if the whole world in all its fields is changing very fast, as is the case today, then the church and the ecumenical movement cannot be exempt. Of course, the goal and the main principles of the ecumenical movement remain valid, but concrete ecumenism takes place in this world and not far away on a star. In this sense there is no doubt: the ecumenical movement stands today at a turning point.

What can we do? How should we proceed? There is no lack of proposals for new methods, new strategies, new paradigms, new conferences, new commissions, new forums and new institutions, proposals involving the wider participation of women, youth and marginalized people. This all may be helpful and positive. But I think we have to dig deeper and to think deeper.

In order to reach a consensus on such deep and longstanding convictions as those held in matters of faith, neither activities – ever new gatherings, conferences, symposiums and public manifestations – nor academic dialogues of experts alone, however important and essential they may be, are sufficient. In order to get matters moving again an impetus is needed which is greater and stronger than human activities and academic conversations can be by their nature. In this situation we have to return to the original impetus of the ecumenical movement. We have not only to commemorate the origins, we have to go back to the origins and to the sources and to draw fresh and refreshing water from them. In its beginning ecumenism was – as we have seen – driven by a spiritual movement, by spiritual ecumenism. We have to renew the original spiritual inspiration.

To many Christians this seems to be an alibi. In some way, however, such a "program" corresponds to the present state of the ecumenical debate. The schisms of the eleventh and of the sixteenth centuries did not occur in response to abstract doctrinal questions. This does not exclude the fact that the divisions were based on a question of truth; but the question of truth historically is always embedded in manifold human conditions, in different concrete experiences of reality, and sometimes hopelessly entangled with them. So Christians did not primarily diverge through discussions and quarrels about different doctrines, but through the way they lived. Different forms of living the Christian faith had become estranged from each other, alienated to the point where they could no longer understand each other, and this led to divisions. Cultural, social, and political conditions and constellations played a role in this process. So to a certain extent, different spiritualities were and are still a reason for the divisions within Christendom.

For a deeper ecumenical understanding and ecumenical agreement a spiritual empathy is needed, an inside understanding of a different and initially strange Christian and ecclesial form of life as well as an intimate understanding from the inside, not just with the mind but with the heart, a sympathy and empathy. Spiritual ecumenism means listening and opening oneself to the demands of the Spirit who also speaks through different forms of piety; it means a readiness to rethink and to convert but also to bear the otherness of the other, requiring tolerance, patience and respect, and not least good will and love which does not boast but rejoices in the truth (1 Corinthians 13:4-6).

On the basis of many experiences in the ecumenical dialogue I can say that ecumenical dialogues only succeed where all of this works to a certain extent. In order to succeed trust must be built and friendships established. Where this is not possible everybody is sufficiently intelligent to find objections to the arguments from the other side. Such dialogues will never come to a conclusion; one could say that they have an eschatological dimension. But when there is friendship and common spiritual ground, the situation changes. This may not lead and normally does not lead to an immediate consensus, but it helps to better understand what the other really means and why a different position is held. It helps to accept the other in his or her otherness.

So for good reasons the Second Vatican Council saw in the ecumenical movement an impulse and work of the Holy Spirit (UR 1; 4). And for good reasons the council called spiritual ecumenism the heart of the ecumenical movement (UR 8). For the unity of the church cannot be made or organised; the unity of the church is the work and the gift of God's Holy Spirit. Only a renewed Pentecost, a renewed outpouring of the Holy Spirit can bestow on us the unity of all the disciples of Christ for which Jesus prayed on the eve of his death on the cross: "That all be one" (John 17:21). Ecumenical work, therefore, can be nothing else than participation in the prayer of Jesus.

Spirituality Invites Discernment

The claim for spiritual ecumenism entails at the same time a danger and a trap. At the present time, spirituality is a much used and ambiguous concept. Often, it has become a mere slogan. For sometimes spirituality is understood in a mere emotional sense and as an escape from and a substitute for an objective confession of faith. This temptation has been present in some enthusiastic movements in the past and in the present as well. Such a spirituality sooner or later becomes empty and void; it cannot help to overcome the differences and becomes ecumenically useless. In order to avoid such misunderstandings we should first try to clarify the term spirituality and the "matter" behind it. Spirituality is a word borrowed from French Catholicism. Literally translated, it means "piety." But this does not cover the whole meaning of the term. The "Ecumenical Dictionary" says that "spirituality is the development of the Christian existence under the guidance of the Holy Spirit." So one can understand spirituality as the Spirit effected way Christians conduct themselves before God. The term signifies a lifestyle guided by the Spirit.

This shows clearly that the term spirituality has two components: the one "from above" which is beyond human reach and is the working of God's Spirit; the other "from below" which takes in human conditions and circumstances in which the Christian existence finds itself, and which it tries to form and permeate spiritually. This places spirituality into the tension between the Holy Spirit who is at work everywhere and in all, and the multiplicity of human cultural and social realities and forms of life. The tension between unity and diversity therefore is rooted in the very nature of the concept of spirituality. Even more, the term spirituality implies the tension and the conflict between the Holy Spirit and the spirit of the world, as it is understood in the Bible.

Spiritual ecumenism therefore is not a magic word which could easily solve the ecumenical questions. Different spiritualities not only carry within themselves the danger of divisions. Spiritualities which are faith incarnate in the world and in culture also carry the danger of syncretism, i.e., the mixing of the Christian faith with religious and cultural elements which do not fit but falsify the faith. Spiritualities can also be linked to political conditions and aims and give to the Christian faith not only a national but also a nationalistic, chauvinist or ideologically pseudo-spiritual character. In some forms of religious fundamentalism this danger is all too obvious. But beside this there also are forms of so-called spirituality, even so-called ecumenical spirituality, which are a mere emotional, empty and void of content, late-bourgeois trivialisation of the Christian faith.

Every spirituality must be questioned about the spirit behind it, whether it is of the Holy Spirit, or the spirit of the world. Spirituality demands the discernment of spirits. Thus, spirituality is not only an emotional affair and does not remove the question of truth, but helps, enables, and even pushes us to seek for the truth. An appeal to spirituality, therefore, does not mean a painless escape from theology. In order to remain healthy spirituality demands theological reflection and theological discernment.

Three Criteria for Discernment

The great masters of the spiritual life have left us a rich treasure of experiences for the discernment of spirits. It is worth rereading them carefully from an ecumenical point of view; much ecumenical benefit could be derived from such a study. But I would like to choose a different, more systematic and theological way and, in three biblical and systematic steps, work out the nature and working of the Spirit and, on the basis of a reflective theology of the Holy Spirit, raise the question of what could be an appropriate spiritual ecumenism.

Creator Spirit

The basic meaning of both the Hebrew and the Greek word for spirit (*ruach, pneuma*) is wind, breath, respiration and – since breathing is the sign of life – life, soul, and finally the spirit as the principle of human life, the place of a person's intellectual perceptions and attitudes of will. However it is not a principle immanent in the human person. Spirit is the life given and empowered by God. God gives it and can withdraw it again. Thus it is God's Spirit which is the creative life force in all things. It is the *spiritus creator* which is at work in the whole reality of creation.

An appropriate doctrine of the Holy Spirit therefore has to start from a universal perspective. It must not hide behind church walls or withdraw into its own inner and innermost self. Pneumatology is only possible in listening to the hints, the expectations, the joys and failures of life, and in marking the signs of the times which are found wherever new life breaks forth and develops, where it ferments and boils, but also where hopes for life are violently destroyed, strangled, gagged or murdered. Wherever true life appears God's Spirit is at work. According to a principle from the late Middle Ages, God has to be found in all things.

A spiritual ecumenism which is shaped by the Bible therefore cannot be one-sidedly introverted or purely ecclesiocentric. Spiritual ecumenism looks beyond itself. Jesus prayed that all be one so that the world may believe (John 17:21). Spiritual ecumenism has to enable the church to give common witness to the world and to bear a more convincing Christian witness within the world. So spiritual ecumenism will have to seek out life and serve life. It must be as much concerned with everyday human life and everyday experiences as with the great questions of human life and survival today, the questions of justice, peace, and of preservation of the creation, but also with human religions and human cultural achievements. However, this does not mean any such thing as secular ecumenism. In order to preserve its own identity and to not become secularist, spiritual ecumenism must be inspired, nourished, and directed by the two other criteria for the discernment of the spirits. This brings me to the second point.

The Spirit in History: The Spirit of Christ

In the Bible the Spirit is not only God's creative power but also God's power over history. It speaks through the prophets and is promised as the messianic spirit (Isaiah 11:2; 42:1). The New Testament announces the coming of the kingdom of freedom in Jesus Christ. He is the creature of the Spirit (Luke 1:35; Matthew 1:18, 20); at his baptism the Spirit descends on him (Mark 1:9-11); the whole of his working on earth is under the sign of the Spirit (Luke 4:14, 18; 10:21; 11:20). The Spirit rests upon him so he can preach good news to the poor, proclaim release to the captives, recovery of sight to the blind, and set at liberty those who are oppressed (Luke 4:18). His resurrection happens in the power of the Spirit (Romans 1:3), and in the power of the Spirit he now is present in church and world. "The Lord is the Spirit" (2 Corinthians 3:17).

Therefore Paul understands the Spirit to be the Spirit of Christ (Romans 8:9; Philippians 1:19), the Spirit of the Lord (2 Corinthians 3:17), and the Spirit of the Son (Galatians 4:6). The confession of Jesus Christ therefore is the essential criterion for the discernment of spirits. "No one speaking by the Spirit of God ever says: 'Jesus be cursed,' and no one can say 'Jesus is Lord' except by the Holy Spirit" (1 Corinthians 12:3).

Christology is therefore the essential criterion for spiritual ecumenism. It counteracts the danger of a spiritual relativism and syncretism which tends to compare the spiritual experiences of the different religions, to mix them up or to choose eclectically from them. It safeguards the uniqueness and the universality of the salvific significance of Jesus Christ. It is opposed to the unrealistic temptation to do without the christological mediation and claim direct access to God. It reminds us that, "No one has ever seen God. The one who is God, who is nearest to the father's heart, he has made it known" (John 1:18). The program of the ecumenical movement for the twenty-first century is the same as for the whole church. Pope John Paul II called it "*ripartire da Cristo*," a new start from Christ.

Spiritual ecumenism therefore will be primarily a biblical spirituality, and will express itself in the common reading and study of the Bible. Saint Jerome tells us: "Ignorance of the Scriptures is ignorance of Christ" (cited in *DV* 25). Therefore the old tradition of *lectio divina* – prayer accompanied by private or common reading of the Bible – is worth renewing. Spiritual ecumenism will always ponder the biblical accounts of the coming of Jesus, of his liberating message and his freeing and healing acts, of his service for others, his kenosis unto death, the whole of his person and his work, and use them as its criteria.

Jesus Christ is present through Word and sacrament. Spiritual ecumenism therefore will be also sacramental spirituality. It is based on common baptism, by which we are already now through the one Spirit members in the one body of Christ and live in a profound spiritual communion (1 Corinthians 12:13; Galatians 3:28).

By baptism we participate in the death and resurrection of Christ (Romans 6:3-5), we become new creatures (2 Corinthians 5:17; Galatians 6:15), we have a new birth into hope (1 Peter 1:3), and are called to permanent spiritual renewal of our life, to a life not according to the spirit of the world but according to the Spirit of Jesus Christ. Renewal of our baptismal vows and liturgical commemoration of baptism is therefore a basic element of spiritual ecumenism.

Baptism tends to eucharistic sharing. By the one eucharistic bread we become one ecclesial body (1 Corinthians 10:17). This participation withstands all divisions (1 Corinthians 11:17-22). It is therefore a deep pain for all who are engaged in the ecumenical movement that normally they cannot share at the Lord's table. This suffering of so many Christians must be a further impulse for all who are responsible for promoting Christian unity.

Finally, like Jesus, we can and may, in the Spirit, say "Abba, Father" to God (Romans 8:15, 26f; Galatians 4:6). Spiritual ecumenism, therefore, is a spirituality of prayer which is centred around the "Week of Prayer for Christian Unity." Like Mary and the Apostles, and with them, it will always gather people to pray for the coming of the Spirit which will unite the peoples in one language, pray for a renewed Pentecost (Acts 1:13f). We join with Jesus in his prayer on the eve of his death "That all be one" (John 17:21).

The Spirit and the Church

Besides the christological criterion there also was for Paul the ecclesiological criterion. Perhaps this is ecumenically the most difficult but also the most urgent criterion. Paul links the Spirit with the building up of the congregation and with service in the church. The Spirit is given for the general good; the different gifts of the Spirit therefore have to serve each other (1 Corinthians 12:4-30). The Spirit is given to all believers and to the church as a whole. As a whole the church is the temple of the Spirit (1 Corinthians 3:16-17; 2 Corinthians 2:16; Ephesians 2:21) built up by all the faithful who are like living stones (1 Peter 2:5). So the acting of the Spirit can neither be confined to the institutions of the church, nor can the Spirit or the charisms be seen to be separate from the ministries of the church, which too are gifts of the Spirit. The Spirit acts not through opposition to each other but in togetherness and in working for each other. He is the enemy of every one when it comes to partisan business and to the forming of factions. The highest gift of the Spirit is love, without which all other charisms are worth nothing (1 Corinthians 13:1-4, 7).

Spiritual ecumenism therefore is ecclesial spirituality. The ecumenical movement did not and does not start from an ec- clesiological and dogmatic relativism and liberalism, which no longer cares about the different church traditions. On the contrary, spiritual ecumenism suffers from the wounds caused by the divi- sions within the church, divisions from which the church bleeds. Thus it reminds the churches not to withdraw into a confessional self-sufficiency, but to undertake courageously all possible and responsible steps to promote Christian unity. Spiritual ecumen- ism will therefore be an examination of conscience, in the existing reality of the church, always thinking ahead prophetically.

The ecumenical dialogue is not only an exchange of ideas but an exchange of spiritual gifts and spiritual experiences (*UUS*, 28). Through ecumenical dialogue the work of the Spirit impels us to an ever greater and deeper truth; he leads us into the whole truth (John 16:13). Ecumenical dialogue absolutely does not mean abandoning one's own identity in favour of an ecumenical "hotchpotch." It is a profound misunderstanding to see it as a form of compromising doctrinal relativism. The aim is not to find the lowest common denominator. Ecumenical dialogue aims not at spiritual impoverishment but at mutual spiritual enrichment. In ecumenical dialogue we discover the truth of the other as our own truth. So through the ecumenical dialogue the Spirit leads us into the whole truth; he heals the wounds of our divisions and bestows on us full catholicity.

During recent decades we Catholics have learned a lot from the experiences of our Protestant brothers and sisters about the significance of the Word of God, about Holy Scripture and its exegesis. At present they are learning from our understanding of sacramental signs and from our way of celebrating the liturgy. In ecumenism with the Oriental churches we can learn from their spiritual wealth, and from their respect of the mysterious; we can share our pastoral experiences and our experiences in dealing with the modern world. Thus the church can learn to breathe again with both lungs.

Such an exchange is not possible without a spirituality of communion. Pope John Paul II described such a spirituality of communion which makes us able to share the joys and sufferings of the others, and which implies seeing what is positive in the others, welcoming and prizing it as a gift from God not only for the other but also for ourselves. "A spirituality of communion means, finally, to know how to 'make room' for our brothers and sister, bearing 'each others burdens' (Galatians 6:2) and resisting the selfish temptations which constantly beset us and provoke competition, careerism, distrust and jealousy." Without such a spirituality of communion the external structures of communion "will become mechanisms without a soul, 'masks' of communion rather then its means of expression and growth" (*NMI*, 43).

A Renewed Pentecost

These three criteria for the discernment of the spirits are very broad. They are by no means an inflexible measuring stick. They are not limiting, they open up. They are upheld by the Spirit of love which drives out fear (1 John 4:18) and overcomes the concerns for one's own identity which tend to block, confine, and smother the ecumenical movement. These three criteria make for an ecumenical dynamism and for a dynamic spiritual ecumenism.

In this sense, there is no ecumenism without personal conversion and church renewal (*UR* 7); it leads to the examination of conscience and cannot be separated from personal conversion and the desire for church reform (*UUS* 16; 24f; 83f). When we move closer to Jesus Christ in this way through the exchange of our different confessional experiences and our different circumstances, and grow into the full stature of Jesus Christ (Ephesians 4:13), we become one in Jesus Christ. He is our unity, our reconciliation and our peace (Ephesians 2:14).

The model for Christian and church unity is ultimately grounded in the Trinitarian love between Father, Son and Holy Spirit. This is the archetype of church unity; the unity of the church is like an icon of the Trinity (*LG* 4; *UR* 3). This means that church unity cannot be conceived as a union of big ecclesial entities like a fusion of big worldwide firms. Nor can the unity of the church be some abstract system that, in a lucky hour, is discovered and agreed upon in a theological dialogue. There is no doubt that theological agreement is necessary. But in the end, a consensus is the work of the Holy Spirit. It does not just drop from the sky. It has to be prepared by many initial consensus processes on the different levels. Through them, and through the disputes that they cause, the Spirit of God prepares the unity of the Christians. But when, where and how unity will happen is in God's providence. It is not up to us to set dead-lines; he alone determines the time. Here the insight of Paul Couturier remains valid. In this Week of Prayer we pray for a unity of the church, "as Christ wishes and by the means which he desires."

Ecumenism was from its very beginning a spiritual happening. Where in the meantime ecumenical consensus has been possible, it has always been experienced as a spiritual gift. A future consensus of the universal church, in which we hope, can only be given as a renewed Pentecost experience. When he opened the Second Vatican Council with a clear ecumenical perspective, Pope John XXIII spoke about such a new Pentecost. To think that the Spirit would not bring to an end and to fulfilment the work he initiated, would be pusillanimity. Ecumenism needs magnanimity and hope. I am convinced that, as long as we do all we can, God's Spirit will give to us one day this renewed Pentecost.

Chapter Two

Prayer for Christian Unity in the Twentieth Century

JAMES F. PUGLISI

Situating the development of the Week of Prayer for Christian Unity in its context since the mid 1960's allows us to understand how the prompting of the Holy Spirit has enabled the churches to come out of their isolation from one another and the world in which they live. There is a reality about prayer that one needs to take note of, namely, that when we pray we are changed. The witness of history indicates this in the very evolution of the prayer for Christian unity.

In his classes on ecumenism, Yves Congar used to say: "We can pass through the doors of ecumenism only on our knees." What he meant by this is that we should not delude ourselves into thinking that we can "make" or "create" the unity of Christians but that unity is itself a gift from the Triune God's very being to God's creation, especially the church. Praying was the preparation for the possibility to recognize when this gift is being offered and for *carpe diem*, for the seizing of the opportunity to accept it. This meant that in this prayer we are being changed, transformed slowly, and sometimes painfully, to accept what God wants for us and not what we want. The reality calls for a new vision and a new possibility whereby we can let go of what we "think we are making or creating" and to allow ourselves to be transformed into the very gift that God is offering.

For us to consider what has happened to "prayer for unity" since the Second Vatican Council we need to look at this from a point of view which is not purely historical but theological. In this chapter, we will look briefly at a theology of prayer (and specifically prayer for unity), then at how a change of "mindset" has gradually been taking place, what the themes of the prayer for unity have been, prayer for unity as the prayer of Christians in common, prayer for unity at the heart of the ecumenical movement, and finally, what the future holds.

A Theology Of Prayer

St. Paul in his letter to the Romans says, "Likewise the Spirit helps us in our weakness; for we do not know how to pray as we ought, but that very Spirit intercedes with sighs too deep for words" (Romans 8:26, cf. 1 Corinthians 12:3). Prayer is completely the work of God through Christ in the Holy Spirit. In this we can see that praise and intercession are not merely human work, nor the fulfillment of the creature's duty to thank or "win over" God. It is the "work of God (Opus Dei), God's communicating with us, effecting salvation and creating life. Prayer comes down from heaven before it returns to God through us, but not without accomplishing that for which God has sent it out (cf. Isaiah 55:10f). The Christian's prayer is a relationship under the covenant between God and us in Christ. It proceeds from the Holy Spirit and from us. This covenanted communion is the attitude of the person who recognizes him or herself as a creature before the Creator. Prayer glorifies the greatness of the Lord, who has created us, and the omnipotence of the Savior, who delivers us from evil.

Prayer is the act by which I adapt myself to the saving will of God. A "request" is not truly a "prayer" unless it is in communion with the will of God as seen in Christ's demand in the garden: "Abba, Father, for you all things are possible; remove this cup from me; yet, not what I want, but what you want" (Mark 14:36). Pagan prayer seeks to mold the divinity to us while Christian prayer puts oneself in the hands of God who molds us and leads us. This is not a sort of fatalism, but rather Christian prayer always seeks to be in communion with the will of God and to cooperate with God's plan of salvation that surrounds the unfolding of the history of the world. Is not this the very content of the *Lord's Prayer*, a prayer taught to the disciples as the proper prayer of the Christian community?

If we were to try to define the interior attitude of the person who prays, we would see that it is composed of a desire not that things should be this way or that way, but subordinated to the sovereign will of God.[1] Prayer has two poles: on the one hand, the felt need and on the other, the intense desire that it arouses. The person who prays, asks, and at the same time offers him or herself to God so that in and through him or her, the will of God, that is always orientated toward the good and salvation, might be accomplished. In the answering of this prayer (often times in ways not expected by the praying person), God transforms the individual more to the unfolding plan (*mysterion*) of salvation, as the prophet Isaiah says: "For my thoughts are not your thoughts, nor are your ways my ways, says the LORD" (Isaiah 55:8).

What should be of interest here for our subject is the attitude of Jesus toward prayer and in particular the very prayer of Jesus in the history of salvation. The first aspect of Jesus' prayer that is important for the context of prayer for unity is how God finds in Jesus the will and the heart of a man perfectly in communion with God's will. The relationship of Jesus in loving obedience as son to God's plan of salvation is to be noted throughout his earthly life: "And the one who sent me is with me; he has not left me alone, for I always do what is pleasing to him" (John 8:29). This theme of filial devotion has a dogmatic value that is decisive, namely that the plan of God constitutes in Jesus the perfect reality of the filial relationship of humanity with God and enables all of humanity to now participate in this reality so that in Jesus Christ all are able to say unanimously, "Our Father."

The letter to the Hebrews describes the filial relationship of Jesus in terms of loving obedience:

Consequently, when Christ came into the world, he said, "Sacrifices and offerings you have not desired, but a body you have prepared for me; in burnt offerings and sin offerings you have taken no pleasure. Then I said, 'See, God, I have come to do your will, O God' (in the scroll of the book it is written of me)." When he said above, "You have neither desired nor taken pleasure in sacrifices and offerings and burnt offerings and sin offerings" (these are offered according to the law), then he added, "See, I have come to do your will." He abolishes the first in order to establish the second. And it is by God's will that we have been sanctified through the offering of the body of Jesus Christ once for all (Hebrews 10:5-10).

The fulfillment of the Scriptures relates the fact of Christ's passion to the combat concerning the kingdom of God.[2] It is knowing that his hour has come that Jesus hastens to its fulfillment in obedience: "I will no longer talk much with you, for the ruler of this world is coming. He has no power over me; but I do as the Father has commanded me, so that the world may know that I love the Father. Rise, let us be on our way" (John 14:30-31).

It is in Jesus, then, that there exists human consciousness and freedom that are offered to God so that his salvific will could be perfectly deployed in the world. It is the birth pangs of all of creation that awaits full redemption (cf. Romans 8:22-25) that passes through the consciousness and the prayer of the First born of all creation, the Principle, the First born from the dead (Colossians 1:15, 18). He is our unique priest and great celebrant of the world. It is in his sacrificed body, the unique temple (John 2:18-22), that we must enter to pray. Here is where Jesus finds his glory, in that loving filial obedience. His glory is not the fragile, superficial glory of humanity, marked by flattering appreciation of other women and men but it is the approval that the servant-Son finds in the Father[3] and this is in the strict sense, the "glory of the only son" (John 1:14. 18). This is the reason why John realizes that Jesus sees this glory when his Passion begins.

The way the gospels look at the prayer of Jesus is with a certain precision in terms of the object of his requests. What interests us in particular is how the Gospel of John speaks about the object of Jesus' prayer in terms of his own glorification or for the disciples or the church. The Johannine vision of the work of Jesus makes clear the reasons for which Jesus was sent. The key moments expressed are seen in the images utilized such as the grain that must die to be reborn in the harvest. It is also the testament of Jesus expressed by what he will do in his own flesh and that which will be accomplished in his body formed of the faithful. All of this is expressed under the form of prayer, namely the desire or wish expressed in the condition of submission to the Other whose decision is sovereign. In this, the prayer of Jesus is perfectly in conformity to the plan of salvation of God and hence it is always answered: "I knew that you always hear me, but I have said this for the sake of the crowd standing here, so that they may believe that you sent me" (John 11:42).

The prayer that is traditionally cited as being Christ's prayer for unity (John 17:11, 20-23) poses some questions as to whether it is applicable to the division and reunion of Christians or simply to the church and its members. In the latter instance the question of the extension of the church would have to be raised.[4] No matter the response to this question that the exegete may give, this question is ecclesiastically and theologically resolved for us by the usage that is made of this text in an ecumenical sense. Even though the prayer of Jesus for the unity of his followers was said only once, it still remains current not only by the fact that the glorified Lord always intercedes for us (Hebrews 7:25), but by the fact that from heaven where he sits at the right hand of God, he completes that which he did, said, and suffered for our salvation while he was on earth.

How then does our prayer for unity relate to Jesus' prayer for unity? It follows the model that says that what is done in the church and is an exercise, an actualization of that which was announced or instituted in the constitutive period of the history of the People of God. The Decree on Ecumenism (*Unitatis Redintegratio*) presents the prayer for unity as the act "to have frequent recourse to that prayer for the unity of the church which the Savior himself on the eve of his death so fervently appealed to his Father: 'That they may all be one' (John 17:21)."[5] When we pray this prayer we pray for unity in the power of the prayer of the Lord that we actualize in history. A history which is that of the church in its fidelity and its continuity but also a history of the People of God in its faults, its limits, its darkness and failures: the history of our divisions. On the subject of divisions, St. Paul uses the verb "there has to be," indicating by that their place in the concrete plan of salvation (1 Corinthians 11:19).[6] It is at the juncture of our divisions, on the one side, and of ecumenism, on the other, of drama and promise, of sin and grace, of repentance and hope that we realize the prayer of the Lord for the unity of his disciples. Rather it is better to say that the Holy Spirit actualizes in us the prayer of the Lord because it is He who prays in us (*Cf.* Romans 8:15, 25; Galatians 4:6; 1 Corinthians 12:3).

When we pray the prayer of Christ for unity we are transformed and unified by it. This happens not only by those practicing it but also within each one. The prayer for unity, as is true for all prayer, is situated under the influence of the Spirit of God who blows wherever he wills and who forcefully nudges us to partake of the profound life of the church and of souls in the search for God. If it is a question of the renewal of the church and of the conversion of heart (*UR* 6 and 7), then the prayer for unity, above all done together, will attain a certain level of truth and profundity. It is in this context that one may begin to speak of a change of mindset from one where we are all estranged from one another to one that requires a communion of mind and heart, namely with that of Christ himself.

A Change Of "Mindset"

In the twentieth century there were two major thrusts in movements of prayer for the unity of Christians. One began in 1908 by

Paul James Francis Wattson, s.a. (1863-1940) the co-founder of the Society of the Atonement with Lurana Mary Francis White, s.a, the other by a French Catholic priest from Lyons, Paul Couturier (1881-1953) in 1935. However, before considering these let us look briefly at what preceded them.

Attitudes of prayer for unity

Prayers were always offered for Christian unity within the Church. All of the official liturgies of the ancient churches of the East and the West contained prayers for unity usually concerning their communion within the same ecclesial body. Later on, prayer dedicated to the Holy Spirit's role in bringing about the unity and renewal of Christians may be noted in the writings of several influential individuals.[7] Perhaps the first formal proposal for united prayer was made by an Anglican priest, Ignatius Spencer in 1840. It seems that there was considerable discussion among some of the members of the Oxford movement on this issue. Key actors included John Henry Newman and Edward Pusey. However, there was not much enthusiasm shown for this "union of prayer for unity" that Spencer proposed even though a plan for united prayer was eventually drafted. It found limited use among Anglicans at that time.

Perhaps the very first organized group founded to pray for the unity of Christians was the Association for the Promotion of the Unity of Christendom (APUC) in 1857. It was ecumenical in its make up consisting of Frederick G. Lee (Anglican), Ambrose Phillips de Lisle and A.W. Pugin (Catholics) and in its intention to have Catholics, Orthodox and Anglicans united in a "bond of intercessory prayer." The purpose of the APUC was to have "united prayer that visible unity may be restored to Christendom." In 1864, however, the Holy See forbade Catholics to take any part in this association.

Just about this same time the first Lambeth Conference of the Anglican Communion met (1867). This and all subsequent conferences stressed the need for prayer for the unity of the church.

Interestingly enough, two key times were stressed as having a particular importance for praying for unity, namely Ascension Day and Whitsunday.

In Catholic circles at the end of the nineteenth century, Pope Leo XIII (1878-1903) was concerned about the unity of Christians. In 1894, he encouraged Catholics to pray the rosary for the intention of Christian unity. One of his concerns was also in regards to unity with Eastern Christians. Hence, in a letter *Provida Matris* (1895), he indicated the use of the novena (nine days of prayers) in preparation of the feast of Pentecost as a time particularly opportune for praying for unity especially for the reunion of Christendom. This plea was repeated in his later encyclical *Divinum illud munus* (1897) on the Holy Spirit where he suggested that the days between Ascension and Pentecost should be devoted to prayer "for the reconciliation with our separated brethren."[8] The two liturgical feasts of Ascension and Pentecost were identified by both Anglican and Roman authorities as being ideal times of prayer for unity.

What may be seen in these diverse appeals for prayer for Christian unity is that there was a certain "mindset" that drove each of these projects. Usually it was either a logic that desired prayer for unity within a certain denominational or confessional body and, in the case of Catholics, a rejoining or return of those who separated from the Roman church. A certain "apologetic" approach may be perceived as being the mindset in place during this period while the churches remained in a certain "blissful" separation from each other – each one believing that it alone was the authentic, true church. One important piece was missing from these positions, namely the ultimate reason for the unity of Christians was mission. At the beginning of the twentieth century we see that the missionary appeal comes to the fore with critical force. This is particularly evidenced in the famous Edinburgh meeting of the World Missionary Conference in 1910 and followed up with the foundation of the International Missionary Council in 1921. These two important events brought the scandalous divisions among

Christians before the world stage. This, added to two major world conflicts, would eventually jolt the churches from their entrenched positions to one of realizing that the Christian vocation has something to do not with myopic concerns but with the salvation of the whole world.

A New Mindset

Paul Wattson, an Episcopalian Franciscan, together with another Anglican priest, Spencer Jones, launched the idea of prayer for unity with Rome. Father Jones preferred the feast of Sts. Peter and Paul, on the twenty-ninth of June. Wattson, however, desired more than a single day dedicated to prayer for unity. He kept the idea of linking it to a commemoration of St. Peter, the feast of the Chair of Peter, then celebrated on the eighteenth of January. In addition, he added another dimension, the missionary one to the understanding of a center of unity. Realizing that the twenty-ninth of June was not only the feast of Peter but also of Paul, Wattson saw and realized the very meaning of John 17: "that they all may be one... so that the world may believe" was in the purpose of the unity that Christ prayed for, namely it was the mission of the church to bring the Good News of salvation to all peoples seen in the mission of the apostle Paul to the gentiles.[9]

This change in mindset is extremely important for the later development that will take place. Up until now, prayer for unity had been conceived of as a call for return to the Mother Church or for unity within one's own church. Here the Spirit was beginning to work a change in attitude. The circle was beginning to widen, even if so little, so as to invite members of other churches to pray a common prayer for full unity. This will come to greater fulfillment with the contribution of Abbé Paul Couturier as the *Chair of Unity Octave* will eventually become a *Universal Week of Prayer for Christian Unity* in 1935.

While Wattson emphasized unity with the Roman church he nevertheless had a particular way of expressing his vision. It was a unity which was seen as being "around the chair of Peter" and not

in submission to it. He believed in reunion but with this understanding of seeing a composite type of unity which did not elimi-
nate all diversity. Unfortunately, once the community of Wattson
entered into full communion with the Church of Rome and with
the absence of an ecclesiology of Rome that allowed this vision, a
"unionist" position quickly developed since this new community
would be under suspicion both from the church that it left and
from the church it joined! Cardinal Jan Willebrands, in a homily
preached during the seventy-fifth anniversary of the founding of
the Society of the Atonement, made the assertion that Wattson's
vision was that of the ancient church and anticipated that of the
Malines conferences which expressed Anglican unity with Rome
as "united but not absorbed."

Earlier in the same century there were other movements of
prayer that had as their goal the unity of Christians. In the forefront
of these was the Protestant Episcopal Church in the United States
which printed a Manual of Prayers for Christian Unity. While these
prayers were destined for everyone it was not anticipated that
Christians would physically pray together but that they would each
in their own places pray for unity. The scope was to provide for
those churches which did not have a liturgical tradition, prayers
that they could use.

Likewise in other Protestant circles there were new proposals for prayer for unity. Developments may be found in the newly
formed Faith and Order Movement. In view of the first world
conference on Faith and Order material was prepared for a week
of prayer for church unity that was to be held during the week
preceding Pentecost in 1921. This week was to be held each year
with Orthodox, Anglican and Protestant participation. The World
Council of Churches' commission on Faith and Order would later
suggest in 1941 that this week be moved to January to coincide
with the Catholic Octave.[10]

A further development or change in mindset took place in the
1930's. The Church Unity Octave was spreading rapidly especially
among Catholics in England, Ireland, Scotland, Belgium, France,

Poland, Italy and the United States thanks to official recognition first for the United States by Pope Pius X. It was then extended universally by Pope Benedict XV with the Brief *Ad perpetuam rei memoriam* (Feb. 25, 1916).[11] In 1932, during a retreat in what is today the Benedictine monastery of Chevetogne, Abbé Paul Couturier prayed over the writings of Dom Lambert Beauduin (1873-1960) and Cardinal Mercier. Couturier was convinced of the need to pray for Christian unity but he was not convinced that the intentions of the Octave allowed others to pray for their return to the Church of Rome, *tout court*. For the first time in 1933, in the chapel of the Assumptionist Sisters in Lyons, he celebrated a reduced form of the Octave, a sort of *triduum* from January 20-22 for the "return of Christians separated from the unity of the church." It was not until 1935 that he expanded his perspective with Orthodox coming to pray together with Catholics as well as inviting other Christians (and non-Christians!) to give lectures on the occasion of these prayer meetings. At the same time he dropped the use of the word "octave" for what he now called the "Universal Week of Prayer for Christian Unity." Couturier always recognized that he was not the originator of this week of prayer but rather the one who broadened it in such a way that others might be able to participate in it.[12] While he based the psychology of this prayer of Christ on John's Gospel he understood that to mean that we prayed for : "*L'Unité que Tu veux par les moyens que Tu voudras.*" This is the prayer that we must pray: not that others may be converted to us, but that we may all be drawn closer to Christ.

As we saw above, there was also a series of prayers proposed by the Faith and Order Movement which went from Ascension to Pentecost. As the Universal Week of Prayer began to catch on in Protestant as well as Catholic circles, the Commission realized that it made sense to move its week to coincide with the time of the two weeks that were proposed by Catholics, namely that of Wattson and of Couturier. Hence in 1941 the dates were changed and from 1958 onwards the material was prepared in collaboration with the Ecumenical Centre "Unité Chrétienne" of Lyons.

The Second Vatican Council

With the event of the Second Vatican Council a new era dawned that was driven by a new mindset. With article 8 of *Unitatis Redintegratio* this new mindset is articulated thus: "it is allowable, indeed desirable that Catholics should join in prayer with their separated brethren." At least for the Catholic Church there was a new spirit and attitude not only toward praying together for unity but also toward the goal of that prayer, namely the unity of Christians for the sake of the mission of the one Church of Christ. In addition to prayers for unity within the Catholic Church the Council now establishes the desirability of prayers together, *in common* for the unity of Christians. The rationale for this is cited from the biblical context of Matthew's Gospel (18:19-20): "Again, truly I tell you, if two of you agree on earth about anything you ask, it will be done for you by my Father in heaven. For where two or three are gathered in my name, I am there among them." The efficacy of this prayer then is seen in the concordance of wills and hence the reason for *praying together*.

In addition the Council gives more theological and pastoral reasons for sustaining praying together for unity. In the Dogmatic Constitution on the Church (*Lumen Gentium*), the Council affirms why Catholics and other Christians can pray together. These reasons are multiple as the Constitution declares: "The Church recognizes that in many ways she is linked with those who, being baptized, are honored with the name of Christian, though they do not profess the faith in its entirety or do not preserve unity of communion with the Successor of Peter."[13] The many reasons listed include: Sacred Scripture, veneration of the Trinity and faith in Christ, the Son of God and Savior, baptism and other sacraments, the episcopate, the Holy Eucharist and devotion toward the Virgin Mother of God. Finally, there is a recognition that in spite of our divisions we can join in prayer and spiritual benefits and that "in some real way they are joined with us in the Holy Spirit, for to them too he gives his gifts and graces whereby he is operative among them with his sanctifying power. Some indeed he has strengthened to the extent of the shedding of their blood" (*LG* 15).

In the years following the Second Vatican Council, many initiatives have taken place in common prayer in all churches and ecclesial communities. It is sufficient to name only some of these to show how diverse and many they are. There is the women's prayer movement which is completely ecumenical that has brought women together not only from diverse ecclesial contexts but from diverse cultural and ethnic backgrounds. Various youth organizations such as the YMCA and YWCA have promoted common prayer and prayer for unity as well as the international youth days begun under the pontificate of John Paul II. Peace movements and churches that are known as "peace churches" such the Mennonites have promoted prayer in common as have many aboriginal groups that have sustained common prayer in an ecological or creational context. In particular, we also mention religious groups like the Franciscans or Benedictines[14] who are not only found within one church but whose movement and prayer forms cross ecclesial boundaries. Finally, we cannot overlook several groups, especially the ecumenical religious communities of Taizé, Bose, Grandchamp, and L'Arche who have promoted an ecumenical spirituality based on prayer in common for the unity of Christians. All of these examples illustrate a change in mindset that has taken place thanks to an awareness of praying Christ's prayer for unity in common that has transformed those who pray for unity into those who live unity in the Spirit.

Themes of the Week of Prayer for Unity

From an understanding of how prayer works within the human person, to seeing how a change in mindset has been effected by the prayer for unity itself, we may turn our attention to look at some of the themes that have been proposed in the past for the Week of Prayer for Christian Unity. The mindset changed from a praying for a *conversion from one flock to another* to praying for a *deeper conversion to Christ*, the true shepherd of the whole flock.

The daily intentions originally proposed for the Church Unity Octave remained fairly unchanged from its inception having the intent to pray for the corporate reunion of separated Christians to the Holy See. These intentions included the following: the return of "other sheep" to the fold, the return of Oriental separatists, the submission of Anglicans, that Lutherans and Continental Protestants find their way back to the Holy church, that Christians in America become one in union with the Chair of St. Peter, the return to the sacraments of lapsed Catholics, the conversion of the Jews, and the missionary conquest of the world.

While the purpose of Wattson's Octave was to pray for the reunion of others to reconstitute unity with the see of Peter, Couturier's general theme was "unity that Christ wills, as he wills, and when he wills." His first scheme made the following suggested intentions for each day: unity of all Christians, sanctification of Catholics, of Orthodox, of Anglicans, of Lutherans, of Calvinists, of all other Protestant Christians, and the unity of all humanity in the charity and truth of Christ. A second scheme proposed in 1946 will add the sanctification of the Jews and the sanctification of all other non-Christians (especially Muslims from 1953) which replaces the sanctification of Lutherans and Calvinists which were grouped together under "all other Protestant Christians."[15] It is interesting to see how the interreligious themes became mixed in with the ecumenical or purely intra Christian relations.

From the time of Paul Couturier's *triduum* until around 1943 there were no specific themes for the week but rather an explanation of what the prayer for unity is. However, starting in 1943 biblical themes were indicated. Some of these themes included: "that they all may be one," "by making peace through the blood of his cross," "the walls of separation do not rise to heaven," "united before the cross," "Orthodox and Protestants, Anglicans and Catholics speak to Christ the Redeemer recognizing their love and sorrowfully repenting their separation," "the love of Christ urges us on," "Jesus, Savior of all," "now in Christ Jesus you who once were far off have been brought near by the blood of Christ.

...He has abolished the wall of separation, thus making peace, ... through the cross, thus putting to death that hostility," "that they may be one as we are one," "one flock, one shepherd," "Christ our hope – and I, when I am lifted up from the earth, will draw all people to myself," "in Christ who prays," "the suffering of separations is in the Prayer for Unity," and "the one who loves his brother lives in light." Between 1959 and 1967 themes were developed in conjunction with the Faith and Order Commission of the World Council of Churches. These included: "be guided by the Spirit," "here is my servant," "I am the light of the world," "I am among you as one who serves," "He is our peace," "great shepherd of the sheep," "behold, I am making all things new," "I will be their God and they will be my people," and "called to one hope."

With greater collaboration between the World Council of Churches and the Catholic Church after the Second Vatican Council, the Week of Prayer for Christian Unity has been planned and is now jointly printed by the Faith and Order Commission and the Pontifical Council for Promoting Christian Unity. Local groups are invited each year to prepare a suggested theme and develop it. It is then given to an international ecumenical group that refines the theme. The joint publication is then sent out to the constituent members of the World Council of Churches and the Catholic Church for local adaptation and distribution. Of the forty-one themes chosen since 1968, all but three have been New Testament texts with the three texts being taken from the Psalms.[16] Overall the emphasis focuses on some dimension of the biblical understanding of unity within the Trinity and our relationship with one another as being made in the image of this "life in communion" with the Trinity. There is always an affirmation that the Church of Christ is one but Christians who are divided from one another need to seek that unity desired by Christ.

Prayer for Unity as the Prayer of Christians in Common

Great progress has been made during the past century. There has been a move from a state where churches did not speak to one another and lived in isolation from each other, to the degree that one might describe the ecclesiastical situation as one of open competition and conflict, to a state where churches now collaborate together in the gospel project. There has always been "prayer for unity" in the life of the churches but the understanding of the meaning of this prayer has changed. Formerly churches prayed for the unity of the church apart from each other. Now Christians pray in common for the unity willed by Christ. This prayer is necessary since it is the way the Spirit is preparing us to receive that very unity for which we pray.

Unity is a gift from the Triune God whose very existence is one. The churches deceive themselves if they believe that they are creating unity or making unity. The united church is not some mega church that women and men are constructing much like the tower of Babel. Rather Christians, in their prayer in common, are learning that very unity that the Spirit is gifting us with. No one knows what the united church will look like except that there will be something of each of us in it. One thing that we do know is that we need to be prepared to accept the gift of unity from God when we are prepared to receive it. Much like the apostles, who on that Pentecost day were surprised by the workings of the Spirit in them, we, too, must be prepared to be surprised by the Spirit and overwhelmed by the Spirit's promptings. We need to remember that they were blockaded behind doors for fear and it was the Spirit who unlocked the doors for them to boldly proclaim what God had done. This was the beginning of realization of the gospel mission. This is where the experience of Babel was reversed. The gospel project then is the continuation of the Spirit's undoing of Babel in the world today.

The Prayer for Unity at the Heart of the Ecumenical Movement

"There can be no ecumenism worthy of the name without a change of heart" (*UR* 7). This change of heart has been exemplified first and foremost by the change that has occurred in the way that Christians pray for unity. When one has prayed with others no one remains the same. The nature of our prayer for unity has changed. Instead of praying apart we now have prayer in common. In an historic consultation between the then Secretariat for Promoting Christian Unity and the World Council of Churches' Commission on Faith and Order in October 1966, there was complete agreement that prayer in common for Christian unity was not only feasible but that it should be jointly planned by both organizations.[17] Until that moment various ecumenical centers were preparing the materials for the Week of Prayer. From an historical point of view it was recognized that Christians prayed for unity for eight days in January due to Paul Wattson, founder of the Chair of Unity Octave, and that all Christians are now able to pray together in a common, universal, Week of Prayer due to Abbé Paul Couturier.

The concrete results of the Second Vatican Council have enabled Catholic Christians to be more actively engaged in common prayer and has recommended their full and active participation in the activity of common prayer. This is considered by many to have become the heart of spiritual ecumenism. The *Ecumenical Directory* speaks of the heart of the ecumenical movement in this way:

> In the ecumenical movement it is necessary to give priority to conversion of heart, spiritual life and its renewal. "This change of heart and holiness of life, along with public and private prayer for the unity of Christians, should be regarded as the soul of the whole ecumenical movement and can rightly be called 'spiritual ecumenism.'" Individual Christians, therefore, insofar as they live a genuine spiritual life with Christ the Savior as its center and the glory of God the Father as its goal, can always and everywhere share deeply in the ecumenical movement, witnessing to the gospel of Christ with their lives.[18]

John Paul II, in following the line of the Council and the *Ecumenical Directory*, speaks of the "primacy of prayer." For him this primacy was expressed on many occasions during his ecumenical pilgrimages and at St. Peter's itself where his experience of prayer in common or "ecumenical prayer" with Christians separated from one another was a source of hope:

> "Ecumenical" prayer, as the prayer of brothers and sisters, expresses all this. Precisely because they are separated from one another, they meet in Christ with all the more hope, entrusting to him the future of their unity and their communion. Here too we can appropriately apply the teaching of the Council: "The Lord Jesus, when he prayed to the Father 'that all may be one...as we are one' (John 17:21-22), opened up vistas closed to human reason. For he implied a certain likeness between the union of the Divine Persons, and the union of God's children in truth and charity" (*UR* 4). The change of heart which is the essential condition for every authentic search for unity flows from prayer and its realization is guided by prayer.[19]

What the Future Holds

Ecumenical dialogues that started in earnest after the Second Vatican Council have had the principle of starting from a confirmation of what we have in common so as to build a strong foundation to deal with the issues that deeply divide us. These dialogues have gone a long way in clarifying and making more explicit what it is that unites us. As the churches focus more and more on the thorny issues which indeed do divide us we will need to stop and meditate in common prayer on the unity that we already have so as to be able to continue the dialogue on those issues which still divide us. We have reached that stage of the dialogue where such issues as the understanding of the doctrine of the church must be discussed.[20] In a certain respect all of the dialogues have been preparing for dealing with these issues as a final resolution of what still separates us as Christians. This is one of the reasons why prayer for unity is so essential and necessary as we go forward. Since many of the issues which the churches will discuss today touch on the very heart of what it means to be church we will need to be centered in prayer, in discerning **together** what is the will of the Lord for us today. This can only be done when we can put on the mind of Jesus who prays in us with his Spirit for that unity which God desires for all of humanity.

This means that discussions about whether the Week of Prayer for Christian Unity takes place in January or preceding Pentecost are not important. What appears to be more important now is that just a week is not enough! Our common prayer for unity must become a daily exercise, even a spiritual discipline. This prayer for unity must now become an integral part of our spirituality. By our baptism, we take on the commitment to seek the unity that God wills for God's people. If we are truly to be made over in God's image and likeness, then our unity as Christians must be an essential element of our identity.

The apostles, when confronting the first major crisis of whether or not non Jews could indeed become Christ's followers without accepting all of the prescriptions of Judaism, came up with a solution, a way forward, which has been cited more recently in our ecumenical discussions: that of placing no burden greater than what the gospel requires (*cf.* Acts 15:28).[21] Is it not time then that we, like those first apostles and elders, had a serious discussion on what are burdens "greater than the gospel requires"? This can only be done in the context of prayer for unity. For just as those apostles realized their solution together with the Holy Spirit, together we must discern what it is that the gospel requires of us in and through the Holy Spirit who prays through us.

Now, more than any other period in the history of the church, is this prayer for unity necessary. Christians are facing new challenges of how to live concretely their faith in the world. In a certain respect then the context within which Jesus offered that first prayer for unity is not so different from ours today:

I have given them your word, and the world has hated them because they do not belong to the world, just as I do not belong to the world. I am not asking you to take them out of the world, but I ask you to protect them from the evil one. They do not belong to the world, just as I do not belong to the world. Sanctify them in the truth; your word is truth. As you have sent me into the world, so I have sent them into the world. And for their sakes I sanctify myself, so that they also may be sanctified in truth. I ask not only on behalf of these, but also on behalf of those who will believe in me through their word, that they may all be one. As you, Father, are in me and I am in you, may they also be in us, so that the world may believe that you have sent me. The glory that you have given me I have given them, so that they may be one, as we are one, I in them and you in me, that they may become completely one, so that the world may know that you have sent me and have loved them even as you have loved me. Father, I desire that those also, whom you have given me, may be with me where I am, to see my glory, which you have given me because you loved me before the foundation of the world. Righteous Father, the world does not know you, but I know you; and these know that you have sent me. I made your name known to them, and I will make it known, so that the love with which you have loved me may be in them, and I in them (John 17:14-26).

This prayer for unity needs to be situated theologically within the type of "*communicatio in sacris*" that is neither sacramental nor liturgical. Paul VI in speaking about the mystery of the church says:

Even before it takes historical shape, the church is one in God's plan that Christ has begun in the gospel and that he goes about unfolding in time, and resolving in the mysterious kingdom of the afterlife. It is one because it is His church, and it is one because it is the object of its redemptive mission that, according to Christ's supreme prayer, aims at making us all one: *ut unum sint* (John 17:21).[22]

Appendix

1968 To the praise of his glory (Ephesians 1:14)

1969 Called to freedom (Galatians 5:13)

1970 We are fellow workers for God (1 Corinthians 3:9)

1971 ...and the communion of the Holy Spirit (2 Corinthians 13:13)

1972 I give you a new commandment (John 13:34)

1973 Lord, teach us to pray (Luke 11:1)

1974 That every tongue confess: Jesus Christ is Lord (Philippians 2:1-13)

1975 God's purpose: all things in Christ (Ephesians 1:3-10)

1976 We shall be like him (1 John 3:2) or, Called to become what we are

1977 Enduring together in hope (Romans 5:1-5)

1978 No longer strangers (Ephesians 2:13-22)

1979 Serve one another to the glory of God (l Peter 4:7-11)

1980 Your kingdom come (Matthew 6:10)

1981 One Spirit - many gifts - one body (1 Corinthians 12:3b-13)

1982 May all find their home in you, O Lord (Psalm 84)

1983 Jesus Christ - the Life of the World (1 John 1:1-4)

1984 Called to be one through the cross of our Lord (1 Corinthians 2:2 and Colossians 1:20)

1985 From death to life with Christ (Ephesians 2:4-7)

1986 You shall be my witnesses (Acts 1:6-8)

1987 United in Christ - a New Creation (2 Corinthians 5:17-6:4a)

1988 The love of God casts out fear (1 John 4:18)

1989 Building community: one body in Christ (Romans 12:5-6a)

1990 That they all may be one...That the world may believe (John 17)

1991 Praise the Lord, all you nations! (Psalm 117 and Romans 15:5-13)

1992 I am with you always ... Go, therefore (Matthew 28:16-20)

1993 Bearing the fruit of the Spirit for Christian unity (Galatians 5:22-23)

1994 The household of God: called to be one in heart and mind (Acts 4:23-37)

1995   Koinonia: communion in God and with one another (John
        15:1-17)

1996   Behold, I stand at the door and knock (Revelation 3:14-22)

1997   We entreat you on behalf of Christ, be reconciled to God (2
        Corinthians 5:20)

1998   The Spirit helps us in our weakness (Romans 8:14-27)

1999   He will dwell with them as their God, they will be his peoples
        (Revelation 21:1-7)

2000   Blessed be God who has blessed us in Christ (Ephesians
        1:3-14)

2001   I am the Way, and the Truth, and the Life (John 14:1-6)

2002   For with you is the fountain of life (Psalm 36:5-9)

2003   We have this treasure in clay jars (2 Corinthians 4:4-18)

2004   My peace I give to you (John 14:23-31; John 14:27)

2005   Christ, the one foundation of the church (1 Corinthians
        3:1-23)

2006   Where two or three are gathered in my name, there I am
        among them (Matthew 18:18-20)

2007   He even makes the deaf to hear and the mute to speak (Mark
        7:31-37)

2008   Pray without ceasing (1 Thessalonians 5:[12a] 13b-18)

Chapter Three

Praying for Christian Unity: the Anglican Tradition

CHARLES SHERLOCK

The Anglican tradition has a mixed record when it comes to praying for Christian unity. On the one hand, a few individual Anglicans have been at the forefront of instigating and supporting the introduction of corporate prayer for unity, leading to its general adoption in the twentieth century. On the other hand, it needs to be acknowledged that the Church of England for centuries protected its privileged standing in England, a position in which such intercession mattered little. This paper seeks to examine initially the meaning and nature of prayer for unity in the latter context, before proceeding to trace the emergence of more positive attitudes and practice.[1]

No Anglican would agree that the Church of England began with Henry VIII (1509-1547). Its separate identity in terms of governance, however, arose from Henry's move from 1529 to repudiate papal authority in England, having himself declared as "supreme head" of the Church of England. Internationally, he aimed to steer a middle way between the continental powers – Rome, the Emperor, the Lutheran princes and Calvinist city-states.[2] The prayer life of the Church of England remained largely as it had been for centuries, though Henry's rejection of pilgrimage and the dissolution of the monasteries (1536-1540) meant that the local focus of spiritual life in England shifted to parish and collegiate churches. Tensions arose between groups favoring reform (whether of an Erasmian or Protestant kind) and those wishing to retain the tradition (whether under the jurisdiction of the sovereign or the Bishop of Rome) but the Church of England remained a single entity in a unified nation state. The Mass continued unchanged, including intercessions for unity in the people of God, but as prayer for unity of mind, heart and purpose within the one church universal, rather than against the background of churches divided by denomination.

The Anglican Communion has its historical origins in the Church of England. Trade, emigration and colonization led to the export of its spiritual structures around the globe, epitomized in the use of *The Book of Common Prayer*. Some churches, for example those in India and the West Indies, initially continued as overseas outposts of the Church of England. Others had a more independent status: the formation of the United States of America from 1776 saw the question of ecclesial identity raised sharply for members of the former royal colonies of Georgia, Virginia and the Carolinas, and Episcopalians in other colonies. The Protestant Episcopal Church of the Unites States which emerged took its episcopal orders (and version of the *Book of Common Prayer*) from the Episcopal Church of Scotland rather than the Church of England, which had found itself unable to act. As the nineteenth century unfolded, other churches derived from the Church of England gradually began to stand on their own feet, each with a distinct ethos related to its origins and context: Canada, South Africa, West Africa, Australia, and New Zealand.

The emergence of the Anglican Communion (as it came to be called from the early nineteenth century) was closely connected to growth in awareness that disunity between the churches needed attention. It is important to appreciate the reality of this fairly recent history, and not "read back" the notion of an "Anglican tradition" into earlier periods. The roots of this tradition, nevertheless, lie in the identity of the Church of England in its formative period, the English Reformation. We therefore turn first to consider the place of prayer for Christian unity as understood in that period.

Prayer for Christian Unity: the English Reformation

When Edward VI (1547-1553) ascended the English throne, reformation proceeded apace, going beyond asserting English independence of Rome to removing images from church buildings, encouraging clergy to marry, and especially introducing a vernacular liturgy. One outcome of the Reformation was the principle of *cuius regio, cuius religio* [where you live determines your religion]: that England (with Wales and Scotland) is an island enabled a neater application of this than was able to be worked out on the continent. Prayer for unity in the church was thus all of a piece with prayer for unity in the nation: in successive versions the *Book of Common Prayer's* prayer for unity consequently focuses on the church generally, rather than on the reunion of rival traditions. Thus in the prayer for the church the petition is for God "to inspire continually the universal church with the spirit of truth, unity and concord."[3] Nevertheless, the prayer continues, "And grant that all they that do confess thy holy name, may agree in the truth of thy holy word, and live in unity and godly love." This reflects the reality that even in a unified national church there will be a lesser degree of practical unity than is the ideal, whether at congregational or wider levels.[4]

Such prayer for unity in the national Church of England was inseparable from prayer for the nation to hold together under the sovereign. Significant place is thus given in each *Book of Common Prayer* to prayer for the monarch, whether as "supreme head" (as Henry VIII and Edward VI were titled) or "supreme governor" (as Elizabeth and her successors are known), with greater place given to prayer for other nations and rulers as time moved on. The petition in the litany, "That it may please thee to give to all nations unity, peace and concord" remains constant in all versions of the *Book of Common Prayer*. In the prayer for the church, however, the petitions cited above are immediately followed in 1549 by prayer for Edward VI, and no other ruler. In 1552 this petition is introduced by a new clause, namely, "We beseech thee also to save and defend all Christian Kings, Princes and governors, and specially thy servant Edward our King, that under him we may be godly and quietly governed" (wording which continues in successive editions of the *Book of Common Prayer*, with the name of the monarch changing). The Catechism, taught to generations of Church of England children from 1549 on, plays its part in reinforcing such prayer: "My duty towards my neighbour" includes "to honour and obey the king and his ministers." To assert, let alone attempt to live out, the idea that there could be more than one church in England was seen as treasonous, because it meant contesting the claims of the monarch.

Elizabeth's long reign (1558-1603), following Mary's attempt to return England to Rome, saw a number of external threats occasioned by continental powers seeking to bring the island back under papal authority. Successive crises saw special prayers being issued, petitioning God to save nation, sovereign and church (entities assumed to be inseparable) from external invasion (notably the Armada, 1588, for which five prayers were issued, and the sea expeditions against Cadiz in 1595 and 1597, calling forth four prayers). Similar prayers were issued in response to internal rebellion, notably that of the Welshman, Dr. Parry, in 1585 (four prayers in English, one in Latin) and the Scots' plot in 1586. In these crisis prayers, threats are depicted in the strongest terms as the work of ungodly enemies of God's word and truth. On the other hand, the "Godly Prayers" used regularly in the Queen's household include "A prayer for the concord of Christ's church," being intercessions for the wellbeing and protection of the nation in the face of attacks. At its centre is the petition, "Let the church, the spouse of Christ, deal large spoils of the conquered Sathan (*sic*)," and being "entered into the voyage of salvation" be brought home safely to port. Another "Godly Prayer," the long "Prayer for the whole state of Christ's church," expands on the Holy Communion intercessions, recalling weakness, "assaults of Sathan" and "the violence of our enemies," asking God to "shew thy great mercies upon those our brethren in other countries, which are persecuted, cast into prison, and daily condemned for the testimony of thy truth." The reference may be to Christian realms threatened by the "Turk" (such as Malta, for which prayers were issued in 1565), or the assault on Protestants by Roman Catholic authorities, notably the Bartholomew's Day massacre of Huguenots in 1572. In sum, prayer for "unity and concord" in the Reformation Church of England embraced church and nation as one reality. Prayer for the unity of the church was thus closely interwoven with prayer for the nation, as personified in the sovereign, which itself was all of a piece with prayer for protection from assault, whether by Christian or other forces.

Prayer for Christian Unity: Restoration and Empire

Elizabeth reigned knowing that her subjects' religious sympathies ranged from English forms of Roman Catholicism to those who wanted "root and branch" reform of the national church. Her successor, James I (1603-1627) brought together divines of a variety of viewpoints at Hampton Court (1604), resulting in a lightly amended *Book of Common Prayer*, and the publication of the Authorized Version of the Bible (1611). James maintained a long-standing commitment to Christian unity in Europe, but this is not reflected in the official prayers of the Church of England.[5] Prayer for unity continued to take the form of prayer for the concord of the church universal, and the existential wellbeing of the church at the local level, closely associated with prayer for the peace and godly quietness of the realm.

Under James' successor, Charles I, the cracks within the nation – religious on the surface, but reflecting wider social and class divisions – broke out into civil war. The immediate winners, those opposing the monarchy, abolished the *Book of Common Prayer* and the bishops' office, but the notion of "one nation / one national church" remained, albeit in Presbyterian-cum-Independent form. It was now the turn of those for whom monarchy, prayer book, and bishop were all of a piece to experience repression. The Restoration of the monarchy under Charles II in 1661 began with the hope of some toleration as regards religious practice, but this soon faded.

The 1662 *Book of Common Prayer* (based more on 1604 than 1637) was to become the standard version for the next three centuries. In the Preface, the revisers claimed that

> our general aim therefore in this undertaking was, not to gratify this or that party in any of their unreasonable demands; but to do that, which to our best understandings we conceived might most tend to the conservation of Peace and Unity in the Church; the procuring of Reverence, and exciting of Piety and Devotion in the publick Worship of God; and the cutting off occasion for them that seek occasion of cavil or quarrel against the Liturgy of the Church. [6]

In this claim, the attitude towards those who differed stands out: the book is the outcome of what "we" conceived. The Preface breathes a spirit of no compromise: any who disagreed (including those who could accept the book's contents, but not its imposition) are dismissed as being "vain," "impetuous," "mischievous," "given to change," driven by "private fancies and interests," of "factious, peevish, and perverse spirits." Some 1,760 clergy were excluded from their livings, and suffered considerably under the Clarendon Code. As a result, the Church of England was no longer comprehensive of the English people. Not only Roman Catholics, but a variety of Dissenters and Non-Conformists were excluded from the established church, meaning also that they were shut off from the universities and public life.

It is against this background that prayer for unity in the 1662 *Book of Common Prayer* must be evaluated. The relevant prayers in the Holy Communion and the litany continued unchanged, as noted above, but with a somewhat different field of reference. One prayer added in 1662, "for all conditions of men," petitions God

> for the good estate of the Catholick Church; that it may be so guided and governed by thy good Spirit, that all who profess and call themselves Christians may be led into the way of truth, and hold the faith in unity of spirit, in the bond of peace, and in righteousness of life.

This prayer is similar to the older forms, and refers primarily to the church universal. Nevertheless, its phrasing suggests that truth, unity and peace were not characteristics fully known in the English situation. It is perhaps the first glimpse of Anglican prayer for unity among churches in the one place – what in the nineteenth century came to be called "prayer for Home Reunion."

The Glorious Revolution in 1688, bringing Dutch couple William and Mary to England, led to greater contact between continental Reformed Churches and the Church of England, improving its relations with Dissenters. The Toleration Act of 1689 ended their persecution, and provided for them to own meeting houses and conduct public worship. In the Accession Service appended to, but not part of, the *Book of Common Prayer*, this fine "Prayer for Unity" was added in 1715 when Anne came to the throne: it was taken up widely from the mid-nineteenth century.[7]

> O God, the Father of our Lord Jesus Christ, our only Saviour, the Prince of Peace;
> Give us grace seriously to lay to heart the great dangers we are in by our unhappy divisions. Take away all hatred and prejudice, and whatsoever may hinder us from godly Union and Concord; that, as there is one Body, and one Spirit, and one Hope of our Calling, one Lord, one Faith, one Baptism, one God and Father of us all, so we may henceforth be all of one heart, and of one soul, united in one holy bond of Truth and Peace, of Faith and Charity, and may with one mind and one mouth glorify thee; through Jesus Christ our Lord. Amen.

But not until 1828 was the Test Act (requiring conformity to particular eucharistic doctrine) repealed, and Reform Bills allowed those who were not communicant members of the Church of England to enter parliament or the civil service. The Evangelical revivals from the mid-eighteenth century furthered spiritual understanding between individual believers, spawning numerous voluntary societies whose membership crossed ecclesial boundaries. Yet prayer between people of different churches was problematic: not until 1849 did the Bible Society have prayer at its committee meetings.[8] Given the general intransigence between English-speaking churches, it is not surprising that prayer for unity was rare. Ruth Rouse notes that "In the last decade of the eighteenth century the call to united prayer was taken up by various churches in the Midlands, especially by Baptists and Independents." Yet "in this movement Christians of different denominations did not as yet pray together, but prayed in groups within the boundaries of their own churches. Meetings of Christians of different churches for united prayer were to come in the nineteenth century."[9]

Overseas, the Church of England had no monopoly on official Christian religion. The New England colonies were founded as Puritan Commonwealths. In these and other American colonies, Episcopalians had to learn to live alongside other traditions. A converse situation can be seen in (what was to become) Australia. The fleet sent to found the New South Wales colony carried a Church of England chaplain, but his presence was a concession wrung from a reluctant English government by Evangelical parliamentarians rather than action by the established church. The convict body included many Roman Catholics and Dissenters as well as members of the Church of England, and Australian colonial governments came to provide stipends for Catholic, Presbyterian and Methodist clergy as well as Church of England chaplains, fostering sectarian rivalry that continued until the 1960s.[10] Such developments can be paralleled in mission churches, bringing ecumenical relationships to the fore, calling for new understandings of both the need for and the nature of prayer for unity, not least within the Anglican Communion. To this we now turn.

Prayer For Christian Unity: New Beginnings For Anglicans

This paper has argued that ongoing prayer for unity in the church universal has been a constant in the Anglican tradition, though what this means changed following the unhappy divisions after 1661. Prayer for unity between divided churches was a relatively new feature. A week of prayer for unity was established by the Evangelical Alliance in the mid-nineteenth century, from the first Sunday of the civil year. Rouse notes that this enabled English churchmen and Dissenters, and in Europe, state church, Free Church and Brethren Christians, to pray together and so come to sense their unity in Christ.[11]

The development in America of prayer for unity arose from the revivals associated particularly with Jonathan Edwards, whose "mantle ... fell on James Haldane Stewart," notes Rouse. A lawyer, ordained in the Church of England, he traveled widely in Europe, and as early as 1821 the Religious Tract Society published his *Hints for a General Union of Christians for Prayer for the Outpouring of the Holy Spirit,* documenting the work of the "Union of Prayer" which he had established for this purpose. Haldane Stewart sought to include people of different Christian traditions in the Union. From at least 1837 he advocated an annual day of prayer, nominating the first Monday of the civil year: Rouse suggests that this probably influenced the Alliance in establishing its week of prayer.[12] She also notes that Haldane Stewart "endeavored, unsuccessfully, to secure Dr. Pusey's support" for the day. Pusey, a key figure in the Tractarian movement, was also diffident about an 1840 proposal for such prayer from Ignatius Spencer, an Anglican convert to Rome.

The Tractarian revival emphasized renewal of the visible church, as well as its individual members. In its circles of influence, prayer for unity included intercessions for the reunion of the churches, though looking in the first place to that between the Church of England and Rome, rather than with Dissenting bodies. As the revival spread, some Church of England clergy moved to Rome, most notably John Henry Newman in 1845, but the resulting personal networks meant that joint prayer for unity became conceivable and possible. In 1857 the Association for the Promotion of the Unity of Christendom formed, with members drawn from the Anglican, Roman Catholic and Greek Orthodox churches.[13] The prayer which the Association commended for use is as follows:

Our Lord Jesus Christ, who saidst unto Thine Apostles, Peace
I leave with you: My Peace I give unto you; regard not my
sins but the faith of Thy Church; and grant her that Peace and
Unity which is agreeable to Thy Will, who liveth and reigneth
for ever and ever. Amen.

The first official Church of England reference to "the Reunion
of the divided members of Christ's Body" would seem to be a mo-
tion passed in 1861 by the clergy of the Convocation of Canterbury.
A decade later, the same body set up a Committee on Reunion. Its
report asked that the Accession "Prayer for Unity" be used in the
Church of England, and that "all classes of Nonconformists should
be invited to institute similar prayers."[14]

Lambeth 1867

Against this background – centuries of refusal to acknowl-
edge other churches in England as equals, participation by some
Evangelical individual members in prayer for Christian unity, and
the limited beginnings of prayer for ecclesial unity in Tractarian
circles – it is refreshing to find the prominent place which the
topic received at the Conference of bishops at Lambeth in 1867.
Indeed, it forms the main subject of the opening section of their
Resolutions, which situates the self understanding of this gathering
of seventy-six (of a possible one hundred and forty-four) bishops
from the British Isles, America, and the colonies:[15]

We, Bishops of Christ's Holy Catholic Church, in visible communion with the United Church of England and Ireland, professing the faith delivered to us in Holy Scripture, maintained
by the Fathers of the English Reformation, now assembled, by
the good providence of God, at the Archiepiscopal Palace of
Lambeth, under the presidency of the Primate of all England,
desire, first, to give hearty thanks to Almighty God for having thus brought us together for common counsel and united
worship; secondly, we desire to express the deep sorrow with
which we view the divided condition of the flock of Christ

throughout the world, ardently longing for the fulfilment of the prayer of our Lord, "That all may be one, as Thou, Father, art in me, and I in Thee, that they also may be one in us, that the world may believe that Thou hast sent me;" and lastly, we do here solemnly record our conviction that unity will be most effectively promoted, by maintaining the faith in its purity and integrity, as taught by the Holy Scriptures, held by the primitive church, summed up in the Creeds, and affirmed by the undisputed General Councils, and by drawing each of us closer together to our common Lord, by giving ourselves to much prayer and intercession, by the cultivation of a spirit of charity, and a love of the Lord's appearing.

This positive attitude towards Christian unity, and especially prayer for such unity, needs to be set in context, however. In the United States, the Protestant Episcopal Church had stood on its own feet since 1784, but the development of colonial dioceses outside England was of more recent origin. The question of how such dispersed, non-established churches related to the mother church, and how missionary dioceses would relate to these, was a live one in the first half of the nineteenth century. Bishops for Cape Town, Adelaide, Melbourne and Newcastle were consecrated in London only in 1847. The Australasian bishops did not meet until 1860 to begin to work on how they should relate to one another and the Church of England. In South Africa, the Bishop of Natal, John Colenso, was deposed in 1863 by Bishop Gray (Cape Town), but he refused to accept this: a bishop recognized by Canterbury was appointed to Natal, and Colenso continued as a bishop of the Church of England in South Africa. How such a dispute could be resolved in a non-established, colonial church was by no means clear, as appeal to the highest English court, the Privy Council, showed. The Canadian Provincial Synod, possibly concerned about the consequences of such a situation in its setting, in 1865 suggested to Archbishop Longley that a "General Council" of all Anglican bodies be called. After spirited discussion in the Church of England, he called all Anglican bishops to meet together.

The 1867 Conference could have concentrated on Anglican affairs, its prayer for unity being intercession that the emerging Anglican Communion might remain one. Yet the "Prospectus of Arrangements" noted by Archbishop Longley in his opening address commences with "The best way of promoting the Reunion of Christendom," and concludes with an appeal for response to this situation.[16] It is noteworthy that only Christendom is specified: missionary movements resulting in rival churches would appear not to be perceived as an issue at this stage. As noted above, the Lambeth bishops strengthened the draft resolution to look beyond the immediate issues facing them and express "deep sorrow" for "the divided condition of the flock of Christ throughout the world." Beyond this Prospectus, however, no Resolution takes up the issue, though the "Address to the Faithful" states, "and we pray that in His good time He would give back unto His whole Church the Blessed gift of Unity in Truth."[17]

Lambeth 1878

The 1867 Conference was not intended to be the first of a series, but after Canadian, West Indian, and American bishops requested a second Conference, the Archbishop of Canterbury called the bishops together in 1878, from which time Lambeth Conferences have met regularly. The 1878 topics and Resolutions concerned the life of the Anglican Communion, yet the committee concerned with "the best mode of maintaining union among the various churches of the Anglican Communion" asked that "this Conference give the weight of its recommendation to the observance throughout the churches of this Communion of a season of prayer for the unity of Christendom." The Conference ruled that in mission situations only one bishop was to be set up, but wider issues of ecclesiology and mission were not in view, and the scope of prayer for unity remained restricted to Christendom.

As regards the date for such a season, the first preference was for St. Andrew (November 30), already observed as a "Day of Intercession for Missions," because evangelism and unity are held together in Christ's prayer of John 17.21-22. But this time "is found to be unsuitable to the circumstances of the church in many parts of the world," so "the Tuesday before Ascension (being a Rogation Day) or any of the seven days after that Tuesday" was proposed.[18] How far this recommendation was taken up across the Communion is difficult to assess, but it represents the most tangible step thus far in the Anglican tradition towards regular prayer for Christian unity.[19] A similar proposal came from the Grindelwald Conferences, held between individuals of differing English churches. In 1892 the members suggested prayer for unity on the first Sunday of each quarter, and in 1894 the consequently Archbishop of Canterbury asked clergy to use the Accession "Prayer for Unity" each Whitsunday (Pentecost).[20]

From Lambeth 1888 to 1920

Several Provinces asked that church unity be on the agenda for 1888, and the Americans proposed what was adopted (with slight changes) as the Lambeth Quadrilateral, a framework for "brotherly conference" with other churches. The latter fell into several groups: Home Reunion (i.e. of "Christian Communions in the English-speaking races"), the Scandinavian churches, Old Catholics and the Eastern churches: each group was discussed in full Reports, with corresponding Resolutions.[21] It is then disconcerting to find that the recommendation of the Committee on Home Reunion, "to pray the Conference to commend the matter of Reunion to the special prayers of all Christian people, both within and (so far as it may rightly do so) without our Communion," is not taken up in the Resolutions.

The Committee Report on Unity from 1897 Conference worked carefully through similar material to that considered in 1888. The outcome, however, was that it "has not been able to propose any resolutions which would bind us to immediate action," though the Conference stated that "every opportunity should be taken to emphasize the Divine purpose of visible unity amongst Christians as a fact of revelation." On the other hand,

Resolution 35 is the first such from a Lambeth Conference: "That this Conference urges the duty of special intercession for the unity of the church in accordance with our Lord's own prayer."[22] These two last affirmations are reiterated by the 1908 Conference, part of twenty detailed Resolutions on church unity, including one suggesting "that private meetings of ministers and laymen of different Christian bodies for common study, discussion and prayer should be frequently held."

Reviewing the discussion thus far, it has been argued that in the Reformation Church of England prayer for unity formed one aspect of intercession for the church universal, offered by a national church. In the context of divided churches, the reality from 1661, such prayer could be seen as offensive, reinforcing the assumption that only the established church was legitimate. By the nineteenth century, in the context of the emerging Anglican Communion, prayer for unity between divided churches started to be a not unfamiliar part of Anglican practice, albeit with Home Reunion and Christendom in view, alongside a strong antipathy to papal claims. The experience of mission churches, attested at the 1910 Edinburgh Conference often credited as the beginning of the modern ecumenical movement, began to open Anglican eyes to a more global, trans-colonial perspective on the nature of Christ's church and its unity.

Prayer for Christian Unity: an Anglican Characteristic

The turning point in Anglican attitudes to Christian unity was the 1920 Lambeth Conference. The bishops' bold "Appeal to all Christian People," deriving from consultations between the Church of England and British Free Church leaders, set ecumenical endeavor at the centre of Anglican self understanding. Unfortunately, looser wording of the fourth point of the Lambeth Quadrilateral, speaking of "ministry acknowledged by every part of the church" rather than "the Historic Episcopate" as part of the necessary framework for reunion, gave (false) hope that intercommunion was possible.[23] Negotiations which followed over 1921-1925 between the Church of England and the Federal Council of Evangelical Free Churches in England went nowhere in practical terms, and impetus for Home Reunion diminished. Though chastened by deeper appreciation of the barriers to be overcome, the vision of a united church in each place remained, as evidenced in strong Anglican support for the initial Faith and Order Conference in 1927. [24]

As regards prayer for Christian unity, however, Lambeth 1920 made no further provision, but growing conflict in the Anglican Communion over liturgy led to definite progress in this area, if not others. The ferment eventuated in a range of new prayer books, in which prayer for unity began to enter the mainstream of the Anglican tradition. The 1912 Scottish *Book of Common Prayer* included the Association and Accession Service prayers, as did the 1918 Canadian revision, and the 1928 "Deposited Book" of the Church of England. [25] From this time onwards, these two prayers (or versions translated into contemporary English) became part of Anglican prayer books.

Anglicans and the Week of Prayer for Christian Unity

In the meantime, a priest of Anglo-catholic persuasion, Spencer Jones, preaching on St. Peter's day, June 29, 1900, suggested that this day might occasion "sermons to be preached on the prerogatives of Peter and Rome as the centre of unity" (definitely a minority opinion among Anglicans at that time!). Publication of the sermon led to correspondence with Paul Wattson, then an Episcopalian priest, who suggested that the octave from January 18 (Chair of Peter – a feast not in the *Book of Common Prayer*, but now included in some Anglican Calendars) to January 25 (Conversion of Paul, observed with propers in the *Book of Common Prayer*) would be a better time, but the papal basis for reunion rendered the proposal unsuitable for widespread Anglican observance. [26] Wattson later became a Roman Catholic priest, and founded the Franciscan Friars of the Atonement, whose vocation to Christian unity gave rise to the Octave of Prayer for Unity from 1908.

In the early 1930s Paul Couturier, a Roman Catholic scholar and ecumenist, was able to reconfigure the purpose of the Octave as intercession for "that peace and unity which were in His mind and purpose, when, on the eve of His Passion, He prayed that all might be one."[27] With this understanding of its purpose, the Week of Prayer for Christian Unity spread to churches from a wide range of Christian traditions. It has been widely observed in the Anglican Communion since World War II, when the formation of the World Council of Churches brought it to the knowledge of congregations. In northern hemisphere provinces it is kept from January 18 to 25; in the southern hemisphere, where January is a holiday month, it is observed from Ascension Day to Pentecost.

In the wake of the liturgical movement and the end of colonialism, Anglican prayer books went through major revisions in the 1970s and 80s. These took into account the revisions being made by other churches, with widespread adoption of the ecumenical prayers texts prepared by the English Language Liturgical Consultation. Some provinces included eucharistic materials on the theme of unity (i.e. specific scripture sentences, introduction to confession, eucharistic preface, post-communion and blessing prayers), and in Australia at least the Week of Prayer for Christian Unity holds a permanent place in the Calendar. Anglicans today pray for unity in conjunction with other churches, alongside regular intercession in their own services for the unity of Christ's church.

One further development has affected Anglican prayer for unity – the enormous shift of attitude towards and by the Roman Catholic Church following the Second Vatican Council. The 1966 visit to Rome of the Archbishop of Canterbury, Michael Ramsey, and especially his praying beside Pope Paul VI, electrified Anglicans to new possibilities.[28] Though the path to unity with Rome is no easy one, participation in joint common prayer, facilitated by the adoption of modern English in both traditions, is now commonplace. In Australia, for example, marked by Catholic-Protestant sectarianism from the first European presence, November 3 is now observed as a "Day for Anglicans and Roman Catholics to pray for one another." The theological work undertaken by the Anglican-Roman Catholic International Commission since 1970 has had common prayer and daily presence at one another's eucharists, at its heart. In sum, prayer in the Anglican tradition for unity now encompasses a new openness to the fullness of the unity for which the Lord Jesus Christ prayed.

Conclusion

This chapter closes with examples of prayers for unity in current use by Anglicans:

Most gracious Father,
we pray for your holy catholic church:
fill it with all truth, and in all truth with all peace;
where it is corrupt, purge it;
where it is in error, direct it;
where anything is amiss, reform it;
where it is right, strengthen and confirm it;
where it is in want, furnish it;
where it is divided, heal it and unite it in your love;
through Jesus Christ our Lord. **Amen.**

From a form used in the intercessions at the Holy Communion:

Father, we pray for your holy catholic church;
> **that we all may be one in Christ.**
Grant that every member of the church may truly
and humbly serve you;
> **that your name may be glorified by everyone.**

From Litanies:

Govern and direct your holy church;
fill it with love and truth;
and grant it that unity which is your will.
  Hear us, good Lord.
Heal the divisions of your church, that all may be one,
so that the world may believe.
  Lord, hear our prayer.

Chapter Four

Spiritual Ecumenism at Vatican Council II

GEORGE H. TAVARD

I n order to understand any historical text it is important, not only to analyze the text in its original language and to see it in its original context, but also to know how it was composed, under whose influences and with what intended purpose. Church historians and historical theologians try to do this with the early councils of the Church, with the medieval councils, with the Council of Trent, and nearer to us, with Vatican Council I.

The same processes should be at work in regard to Vatican Council II. And in this regard we still have the advantage that a few of its officers, members, and theologians are still living. I once recommended that the religious communities which were present at the council, through their bishops, their Superiors general, and eventually some of their theologians, make a study of the activities of these persons during the council, including the theology of their speeches, if any. I have had no great success in this, least of all, I regret to say, in my own congregation, the Augustinians of the Assumption.

At any rate I will try, in the present chapter, to throw light on the specific passages of the Decree On Ecumenism, *Unitatis redintegratio*, with the help of what I remember of the work of the commission that was responsible for it, the Vatican Secretariat for the Promotion of the Unity of Christians.

The Consultants in the Preparatory Period

The bishops at Vatican Council II were assisted by theologians, who were designated by the general title of *periti,* "experts." There were *periti* in the four sessions of the council. Before the first session started their equivalent in the preparatory commissions were called "consultants." In the preparatory commissions the consultants were selected and named by the president of the commission with the assistance of the secretary. Cardinal Augustine Bea (1881-1968) and Monsignor Jan Willebrands (1909-2006), were therefore responsible for the nomination of consultants for the Preparatory Commission on Ecumenism. How they made their selection was never really explained. In principle consultants were chosen either because they were already well known for their ecumenical expertise or, if they were religious, because their community had a lively interest in the unity of Christians. Better known for its ecumenical orientation was the Abbey of Chevetogne in Belgium. In the United States the Paulist Fathers and the Society of the Atonement were well known, the first for their founder's concern for the conversion of America, the second for its commitment to prayer for the unity of Christians. It was therefore normal that there should be Paulists in the Secretariat for the Unity of Christians: Thomas Stransky was an official of the Secretariat, James Cunningham (1901-1994), a former Superior general, who was the Pastor of the American Church in Rome, St. Susanna.

My own community, the Augustinians of the Assumption, which was centered in France, was chiefly known for its work in Eastern Europe, for its interest in the Eastern rites and churches, and for the scholarly work of its Byzantine Institute. My own chief interest, like that of some of our religious in the Netherlands, was in the study of Protestant and Anglican theology. I do know that I was recommended to Cardinal Bea by a German lady who, at the time, lived in Rome, who had spent some ten or more years in the United States, and whom I had met a number of times in New York City at gatherings of Helen Iswolsky's "Third Hour," an informal occasional meeting, originally of Russian Orthodox and Catholics. In the 1950s, it was one of the few places in New York which nurtured a truly ecumenical attitude.[1]

When my name was suggested to him by a person he trusted, Bea, presumably, consulted with Willetrands. I had met Willebrands once in Paris in 1952, in an ecumenical context. And so the Cardinal put me on his list of consultants. Among the Franciscans of the Atonement he selected Edward Hanahoe (d.1994). In 1954, Hanahoe had published a pamphlet which contained what he called "the first official statements in modern times of the stand of the Catholic Church on non-Catholic reunion movements." The documents were the letter *Ad omnes episcopos Angliae*, addressed by Pius IX to the Catholic bishops of England on September 1864, and the letter *Ad quosdam Puseistas Anglicos*, in which the President of the Holy Office, Cardinal Patrizi, replied on November 1865 to a letter signed by nearly 200 clergy of the Church of England. In his preface, Hanahoe had summed up with approval the teaching of these documents: "Reunion means return to communion with the Chair of Peter." He had duly remarked that, in 1919, when Pope Benedict XV received delegates of the Faith and Order movement, and declined their invitation to participate in the international conference that was projected, copies of these texts were given to the delegates.[2] The implication was that the two letters embodied the contemporary official position of the Catholic Church.

In France the archdiocese of Lyon had an ecumenical reputation. Abbé Paul Couturier (1881-1953) and abbé Laurent Remillieux (1882-1949), who initiated the ecumenical dialogues of the "Groupe des Dombes" in 1937, were priests of the archdiocese, Couturier a teacher of English in a Catholic *école secondaire*, Remillieux the pastor of a parish in the city of Lyon, Notre Dame Saint Alban. In addition, Father Maurice Villain (1900-1977), a professor of theology at the theologate of the Marists in Sainte Foy, a suburb of Lyon, was a close friend of abbé Couturier. He was noted for his friendly contacts in the French Reformed Church.[3]

It was normal that someone representing the line of thought of Couturier should be a consultant.

Those who knew Villain, however, were aware of his occasional propensity to become excessively emotional when he was speaking about the attitude of Catholics toward Protestants. So it was not Villain who was chosen as a consultant of the Secretariat for Unity. It was Pierre Michalon (1911-1986), a Sulpician, who had been a director in several seminaries. In 1954, after the death of Couturier, Michalon had founded the *Centre Unité Chrétienne* (today, *Centre Saint Irénée*), in Lyon, in order to continue Couturier's ecumenical apostolate, and to facilitate the annual Week of Prayer in January for the unity of the churches.

Varying Conceptions of Prayer for Unity

Thus it happened that, from the start, two conceptions of the Catholic prayer for Christian unity had its advocates in the Secretariat for the Unity of Christians. The Week of Prayer for Christian unity, initiated by Paul Wattson (1863-1940) and faithfully advocated by the Society of the Atonement which he had founded, was symbolic of the unity between Peter and Paul, since it took place between the Feast of St. Peter's Chair in Rome (January 18) and the Feast of the Conversion of St. Paul (January 25). By the same token, it further symbolized unity between the successor of Peter and those Christians who professed justification by faith alone, as Martin Luther had rediscovered it in meditating on the Epistles of Paul, especially on the Epistle to the Galatians, which he chose of the topic of his University lectures no less than six times, in 1519, 1523, 1525, 1534, 1535, and 1538.[4] The original Church Unity Octave therefore implied praying for the unity of the heirs of the Reformation with the Bishop of Rome. Unfortunately the liturgical reform of Paul VI did away with this symbolism when it suppressed the Feast of the St. Peter's Chair in Rome. Along with their symbolism, the dates of the Week of Prayer have lost their justification.

When thus formulated by a member of the Episcopal Church, this was a bold prayer. Paul Wattson courageously anticipated future times, when the mutual prejudices and recriminations of the past will be, though remembered, totally overcome. He chose to ignore the problems and difficulties that remained if the traditional pontifical authority, modelled on the political model of absolute monarchies, was to be adapted to the conditions of the modern world, in which political authority wants to be democratic. When formulated by those who are already in communion with the Bishop of Rome, however, the prayer for unity that Wattson advocated became a prayer for others, that they may "return" to the Catholic Communion, or "submit" to the Bishop of Rome, successor of Peter. Such a wish was in keeping with the "unionism" of the encyclical of Leo XIII, *Satis cognitum* (1896).

Edward Hanahoe was a fervent advocate of this original form of the prayer for the unity of Christians. He could argue that it was in harmony with the thought of Pius XI in the encyclical, *Mortalium animos*. Now the formulation that was spread in France by Paul Couturier from his center in Lyon was more than a variant. It enabled all willing Christians to pray together for the unity that Christ wills, to be reached according to the means that He wills. It therefore implied an ecclesiology that was contrary to the implicit thrust of canon 1258 (*Code of Canon Law*, 1917), which forbade *communicatio in sacris* with non-Catholics.

Formative Influences

Although I studied theology at the Catholic Faculties of Lyon from 1942 to 1947, including one year of preparation for the pontifical degree of the doctorate in Sacred Theology (S.T.D.), which I received in June 1949, I never met Couturier, who kept a low profile in the archdiocese. I once visited the parish of his friend and associate, Laurent Remillieux, but I did not see the pastor, who did not live close to the church. On occasion I met his devoted friend Villain, who well knew that one of his own students, an Australian, liked to visit with me in order to speak English.

The community where I lived in Lyon was itself ecumenically oriented, but with an interest in Orthodoxy rather than in Protestantism. The older priests, including the Provincial Superior, Maximilian Malvy, who lived with us, had spent a number of years in Bulgaria and Turkey. (We used to have a scholasticate in Kadi Köy, the old Chalcedon, which is in the Asian suburbs of Istanbul). The local Superior, Sévérien Salaville (1881- 1965), who was himself a well known theologian, had lived in Athens and spoke modern Greek quite well. He was author of the article on epiclesis in the *Dictionnaire de Théologie Catholique*, and he had translated Nicholas Cabasilas' *Commentary on the Divine Liturgy* for the collection, *Sources chrétiennes*. He knew Couturier.

Another member of the community, however, was Martin Jugie (1878-1954), famous for a five volume study of Orthodox theology (composed in Latin!), and for a book on the Assumption of the Virgin Mary,[5] which may have had some influence on the definition of the Assumption by Pius XII. Salaville and Jugie, however, had different views of ecumenical relations. Jugie wanted to convert every Christian to Catholicism. Salaville considered the Orthodox Church as a true church, the members of which need not enter individually into communion with the Bishop of Rome. He hoped that the churches would be some day reconciled. He also had good documentation on the World Council of Churches, and he encouraged me to study Protestant and Anglican theology. Martin Jugie remained in the unionist perspective of Leo XIII. He was therefore close to the early concerns of Paul Wattson, although he was not familiar with the American or even the English scene. Salaville's thought, on the contrary, was similar to the spiritual ecumenism of Paul Couturier. Both his experience and his scholarship were with Orthodoxy, not with the Western churches. In private he was quite critical of Jugie's rather negative judgments on the Orthodox Church. He could have agreed with what I later heard Father Alexander Schmemann say: "Jugie is a man who knows everything, and understands nothing!"

In addition to this ecumenical, but divided, environment, the library of our house abounded in documentation about Eastern Europe and about Orthodoxy. Some of our religious had been heavily involved, in the 1920s and 30s, in a truly ecumenical publication, *L'Union des Eglises*, founded in 1922. It had changed its name to *L'Unité de l'Eglise* in 1930, because of the fear that the original title was not in harmony with the orientation of Pius XI's encyclical, *Mortalium animos*, which had been published in 1928, shortly after the Faith and Order Conference of Lausanne (1927). In this encyclical Pius XI had accused Faith and Order of promoting "pan Protestantism." And elsewhere he had praised "the work of the unionistic restoration."[6] Whatever the cause, dwindling readership or theological scruples, *L'Unité de l'Eglise* had folded up by 1937.

In the five years I spent in Lyon the Week of Universal Prayer for the unity of Christians, during the Octave between the Conversion of St. Paul and the Chair of Peter in Antioch, was solemnly celebrated in a well known church, the old Basilica Saint Martin d'Ainay (which had been consecrated by Pope Pascal II, in 1107). It was widely advertised. And the tone was definitely in the spirit of Paul Couturier.

The Secretariat for the Promotion of Christian Unity

The Secretariat for the Promotion of the Unity of Christians was created by John XXIII on June 5, 1960.[7] In the following October sixteen members (mostly bishops, with a few priests also) and twenty consultants were named. The two conceptions of the prayer for unity were duly represented among the members and consultants of the Secretariat. Nobody, however, in the two years of the active preparation of the council, suggested that a choice had to be made between them. Edward Hanahoe at one time presented a few pages in which he explained Paul Wattson's understanding of Week of Prayer. But, as also happened with other documents that came from the initiative of a member or a consultant, we had no general discussion of the text. It was considered to be for information only. When I reflect on the membership of the Secretariat, however, it is clear to me that Hanahoe was not without support for the view that the Catholic prayer for the unity of Christians can only be for the "conversion" of Orthodox and Protestants and their acknowledgement of the primacy of the Bishop of Rome, successor of Peter.

Among the priest members, Charles Boyer, s.j., the future founder and director of the review, *Unitas,* thought along these lines. He was nevertheless eager to develop good relations with the pastoral leaders and with the theologians of Orthodoxy, Anglicanism, and Protestantism; and he was a careful observer of the World Council of Churches. Monsignor Michele Maccarone, a professor of Church History at the Lateran University, was well informed and a clear thinker, but his theology seemed to follow neoscholastic lines that were still close to the Counter Reformation.[8] He was unlikely to approach Protestant thought with understanding. In the Secretariat for Unity he was, rightly or wrongly, suspected of being a spy. In any case he was always listened to carefully, because he also worked with the Theological Commission headed by Cardinal Ottaviani.

The best informed of the priest members about the ecumenical movement was undoubtedly Canon Gustave Thils (1909-2000), a professor at the University of Louvain. He had published a book on "ecumenical theology." He had just composed a very thorough "doctrinal history of the ecumenical movement," which came out in 1963.[9] In the Preparatory Commission, Thils worked chiefly on a text in which he analyzed the "central ecumenical question," namely the existence of the ecumenical movement and of the World Council of Churches, along with reflections on what ought to be the Catholic attitude toward them. This text was not submitted to the council. It provided the basis of the Ecumenical Directory that was issued by the Secretariat for Unity in 1967 and 1971.

Among the bishop members of the Secretariat, the archbishop of Westminster, John Carmel Heenan (1905-1975), who was elected to the Secretariat by the bishops during the council, held a similar position. An early chronicler of the council placed him among the bishops who saw ecumenical dialogue as "an occasion to explain the Catholic truth in its fullness to others, and to bring them to the Catholic Church."[10] In fact, Archbishop Heenan came with little understanding of ecumenism. At the first meeting of the Secretariat which he attended he remarked to me: "We are not doing much for lapsed Catholics, are we?" I replied that our concern was with Christians who were not Catholic; other conciliar commissions might consider the problem of lapsed Catholics, but it was not the task assigned to us. It was Heenan's assumption that Catholic ecumenism was primarily concerned with lapsed Catholics. However, it is fair to add that the archbishop adjusted fast, and well, to the ecumenical opening to which the Vatican Secretariat for the Promotion of the Unity of Christians invited the council.

In reality, few of the members of the Secretariat were familiar with the history of the ecumenical movement. The Bishop of Bruges, Emile Joseph de Smedt (1909-1995), and the Bishop of Lausanne, François Charrière (1893-1976), were the best informed. The Archbishop of Rouen, Cardinal Eugène Martin (1891-1976), was very open. So was William Hart (1904-1992), Bishop of Dunkeld, Scotland, who had good relations with both the Kirk (Calvinist) and the Church of Scotland (Anglican). The Bishop of Umtali (Zimbabwe), Donal Lamont (1911-2003), a Carmelite from Ireland, was fairly knowledgeable on the ecumenical movement, and eager to promote good relations among all Christians in Africa. Angelo Prinetto (1906-1993), vicar apostolic of Loretto, the center of a Marian pilgrimage based on a legend, had a remarkably open mind for ecumenism, but he had no experience of it. Michele Maccarone was well informed, a good historian, and a clear thinker. But he generally favored neoscholastic theology, and and he was unlikely to see non-Catholic thought in a good light. He had a hidden influence because he also worked in the council with the Theological Commission, giving rise to the suspicion that he was spying for Cardinal Ottaviani.

Among the consultants of the Secretariat, Gustave Weigel, s.j., who was truly an ecumenical pioneer among American Catholics, was sympathetic to Hanahoe's position. In a letter he addressed to me on January 18, 1956 he gave a neat summary of his position on ecumenism. Generally he had some mistrust of the Europeans' commitment to the total truth. He suspected that Catholic ecumenists on the Continent were prone to tone down the traditional doctrines when they met with Protestants. He considered the Anglo-Saxons more reliable as witnesses to the Catholic faith. The following quotation gives a glimpse of both his openness and his main concern:

> I agree with you entirely that we must try to understand the psychology of the Protestant. We must know his history. We must recognize the sincerity and fervor of his piety. We must never forget his dedication to God, to Christ and the Word. We must not forget our own errors and our own lack of charity. Yet we must keep one thing clear always. We are humbly asking him to become a Catholic and that means he will be a Protestant no longer. In sincerity and truth we can tell him that he will lose none of the religious values that are so dear to him. Yet the total structure of his values will be changed, by enrichment we insist, but very definitely changed...[11]

In his biography of Weigel, Patrick W. Collins remarks that Weigel occasionally mentioned three solutions to Christian disunion: compromise, comprehension, conversion, to which he later added a fourth, convergence.[12] Conversion was what Weigel hoped for, until he recognized the possibility of ecumenical convergences, which in turn would facilitate eventual conversions. Weigel, meanwhile, had a great desire, and a wonderful capacity, for friendly dialogue with Protestant theologians. He had a special admiration for Paul Tillich, in whom he found a concern that was missing from most Protestant thinkers in America, namely a systematic conception and presentation of doctrines. When the first session of the council was about to start, Cardinal Bea called Weigel to Rome to act as an official interpreter for the English speaking Protestant observers. This choice well reflected the impression that Weigel generally made in the meetings of the Preparatory Commission.

The Conciliar Decree on Ecumenism (*Unitatis Redintegratio*)

Cardinal Bea and Monsignor Willebrands had themselves chosen the consultants of the Preparatory Commission. The task of these consultants, however, came to an end with the beginning of the first session of the council. Bea had no say in the selection of the conciliar *periti*, the theologians who were called by John XXIII to attend the council and to work in its commissions. The choice was presumably made in the Secretariat of State, which worked closely with the pope in the daily task of presiding over the universal church. In any case, I was notified by the Secretary of the council, Pericle Felici (1911- 1982), that I was called to the council as a *peritus*. Cardinal Bea, I was told later, was informed of it when he read the list of conciliar *periti* in the Vatican newspaper, *Osservatore Romano*. During the sessions, the Secretariat for Unity, to which John XXIII gave the status of a conciliar commission, met about once a week. All its consultants who were in Rome could attend, but since they had nothing to do in the council itself, they had little incentive to go to Rome. Only the conciliar *periti* attended the daily sessions and participated in writing the texts to be proposed to the council.

The Decree on Ecumenism (*Unitatis redintegratio*) was the logical place for a treatment of prayer for Christian unity. The task was generally divided between those who would write about Orthodoxy, and those who would write about the churches of the Reformation. Everything was eventually discussed in the whole Secretariat. But the work of composing was done in small groups, occasionally by one person alone. I can give some examples, two of which relate directly to the spiritual dimension of ecumenism. Willebrands formed a subcommittee of five, all of them French speaking, to compose a short text that would fit in chapter two of the decree (The Practice of Ecumenism). The purpose was to put an end to the restrictions of canon 1258 (*Code of Canon Law* 1917) regarding *communicatio in sacris*. I have given the details of this story in a previous publication.[13] It will be enough here to say that the theological principles, formulated in article 8, were enunciated by the future Cardinal Jerôme Hamer, who chaired this small group, and that the Latin formulation was done by myself. Once the group of five had agreed to it, the text was brought to the whole Secretariat, where no one objected to it. When it came to the whole council, however, more than 500 amendments were proposed, which I had to classify and sort out before suggesting what to do with them at a meeting of the Secretariat.

On another occasion Willebrands asked me to propose a short text concerning the confession of sins against unity. He gave no instructions on what to say or how to say it. Clearly, however, any treatment of this point had to avoid suggesting that the church as such has sinned against unity. And it should imply that not all the blame for the past separations can be put on the shoulders of the Reformers, and that Catholics shared the responsibility for the estrangements and schisms. After thinking about it one weekend I wrote a few lines in Latin and brought them to Willebrands, who agreed that they should be incorporated in the chapter. It was adopted without change when chapter three was discussed and approved by the Secretariat.[14]

Another passage can be mentioned. Again, Willebrands invited me to write some lines about ecumenical dialogues on moral questions. Here the challenge was to overcome the not infrequent prejudice of Catholics that Protestants are satisfied with a lax morality. Again, I wrote several lines. They were placed unchanged in article 23. It is unfortunate that the standard American versions of these lines include a major mistranslation, which is not only unfaithful to the official Latin text of the decree, but is also theologically wrong.[15]

I do not know how many other consultants were asked to write specific passages, as these requests were not reported to the entire Secretariat, but only to the subcommittees in charge of the specific chapters of the decree. Yet I know one case that touches our topic directly. Pierre Michalon, as I said above, was close to Paul Couturier. If Maurice Villain, as his favored friend and disciple, had inherited, as it were, Couturier's prophetic mantle, it was Pierre Michalon who, since 1958, continued Couturier's publishing activities, especially by spreading models for the Week of Prayer of January, and through the many *Pages documentaires* which the *Centre Unité Chrétienne* printed and distributed. It was therefore normal that Michalon would be the main contributor to the sections of *Unitatis Redintegratio* concerning spiritual ecumenism. Edward Hanahoe was not present, since he was not among the conciliar *periti*. And those who might have supported his point of view did not feel strongly enough to oppose what Bea and Willebrands clearly considered an important factor in the promotion of Christian unity.

The sections of *Unitatis Redintegratio* in the writing of which Michalon was especially involved are artlicles 7 (Conversion of Heart) and 8 (Prayer in Common). "There is no ecumenism, properly so called, without an interior conversion." The scope of this conversion is described in the next sentence: "The desires for unity are born and they mature from newness of mind, from renunciation of oneself, and from the most free effusion of charity." There follows a personal urge to pray: "Therefore we should implore the Holy Spirit to give us the grace of sincere abnegation, humility, kindness in service, and a fraternal generosity toward .others." Then, after quoting Ephesians 4:1-3, the text points out that this exhortation applies specifically to the ordained. The text that I wrote on sins against unity follows, and a final recommendation: "May all Christians remember that they will promote, and even contribute to, the union of Christians in the measure of their zeal for a life that follows the gospel more purely..." These lines, written mostly under the inspiration of Couturier's advocacy and example, were in perfect harmony with Paul Wattson's constant spiritual concerns.

The beginning of article 8 introduces a typical expression of Paul Couturier, when it says: "This conversion of heart and holiness of life, along with public and private supplication for the unity of Christians, must be considered the soul of the whole ecumenical movement, and may rightly be called spiritual ecumenism." Again, this formulation, which purposefully quoted Couturier ("spiritual ecumenism" as "the soul of the ecumenical movement"), converged with the spiritual dimension of prayer in the life of Paul Wattson and among the Franciscans of the Atonement. The text went on to recommend prayer in common with other Christians. This was of course the place where the older formula for the Octave of Prayer had become obsolete, and where Couturier's formula, though not mentioned in the decree, was necessary. Had he been present when these passages were composed, Father Hanahoe could have had no objection, for the Franciscans of the Atonement remained very much aware of the spiritual depths of their founder. In fact, when the text went to the whole council there were few amendments, and they were inconsequential, as can be seen in the commentary on *Unitatis Redintegratio* by the Archbishop of Paderborn, Cardinal Lorenz Jaeger, who was himself a member of the Secretariat for Unity.[16] Maurice Villain was certainly right when he wrote in his autobiography: "the spirit of abbé Couturier ... left its impression on chapter two of the decree." I doubt he was correct, however, when he claimed that, during the council, Couturier's name "resounded many times under the vaults of St. Peter's."[17] If it did, I never noticed it myself, although I attended all the daily sessions in the gallery reserved to the *periti*, next to that of the Superiors General of Religious Orders.

The Ecumenical Directory (1967, 1970)

The Decree *Unitatis Redintegratio* was followed, in May 1967, by the publication of an Ecumenical Directory, Part One coming out on May 14, 1967,[18] Part Two on April 16, 1970.[19] Part One deals with Ecumenical Commissions, with the validity of baptism, and with several points relating to spiritual ecumenism; Part Two with "Ecumenism in Higher Education." Matters of prayer are touched on in Part One. The Directory mentions "the week from 18-15 January, called the Week of Prayer for Christian Unity."[20] It specifies, "let all pray for unity in a way consonant with Christ's prayer at the Last Supper: that all Christians may achieve 'that fulness of unity which Jesus Christ wishes' (UR 4)."

These two parts were composed by a small group that included the officials of the Secretariat, some of the conciliar *periti* (I was among them), and some lay persons who were already active in ecumenism. As had been the case in the composition of *Unitatis Redintegratio*, nobody wished to oppose Paul Wattson's original project of the Week of Prayer, and Paul Couturier's adjustment on it to the developing ecumenical consciousness of the mid-twentieth century. In the circumstances that followed the creation of the World Council of Churches in 1948, this adjustment could only be seen as an improvement. It was urgent for the Catholic Church to promote a prayer for the unity of Christians in which all Christians can join. This was the intent of the writers of *Unitatis Redintegratio* when they designated "conversion of heart" as the soul of the ecumenical movement, which deserves the name of "spiritual ecumenism" (UR 8).

Chapter Five

Monasticism and Prayer for Christian Unity: The Community of Grandchamp

SISTER MINKE DE VRIES

N estled along the banks of the Areuse River where the waters of the mountains of the Swiss Jura empty into Lake Neuchatel is the tiny hamlet of Grandchamp. This is the home of the Protestant monastic community of Grandchamp, an open contemplative community of women whose life is deeply marked by prayer for Christian unity. The community was born in the confluence of biblical, liturgical, ecumenical, and spiritual movements of renewal, and gives witness today to the convergence between the monastic vocation and prayer for unity. As we shall see, the community's ecumenical vocation is directly linked to the movement of prayer for the Christian unity. This becomes apparent when we consider, first, the influence of Paul Couturier upon the community in the founding years, and subsequently, some aspects of the community's contemporary spirituality. The living experiment in prayer for unity and Christian hospitality of this and other monastic communities can be a rich resource for the churches as they seek to enliven their commitment to "spiritual ecumenism" which the Second Vatican Council has called the "soul" of the ecumenical movement.

The Influence Spiritual Ecumenism
in the Founding Years[1]

The Community of Grandchamp's vocation of prayer was deeply influenced by the founding sisters' contacts with Father Paul Couturier beginning from 1940, at about the same time that they set out together in a common life. They maintained this relationship with Father Couturier until his death in 1953, several months after the first professions of the sisters, an event which he carried in his prayer, though he was gravely ill. A look at the birth of the community, especially at two of its founders, Mother Genviève Micheli and Sister Marguerite de Beaumont, will help us to appreciate the importance of Father Couturier for the sisters' common life today. Further, through a consideration of their correspondence, we will attempt to show how Couturier's message continued to influence the community after his death. This influence has not always been recognized. It is perhaps only because we now have an opportunity to look back over the history of the community that we are able to appreciate more fully the extent to which the spirituality of prayer for unity has marked the community's vocation. As we reflect back on the life of these women, it becomes apparent that the birth of the Community of Grandchamp was not the fruit of a purely human effort. Rather, it was born gradually through the lives of women who were truly open to the Holy Spirit.

Marguerite de Beaumont, originally from Geneva, came to live at Grandchamp in March of 1936. She was invited to Grandchamp by a small group of women from French speaking Switzerland, the Dames de Morges, to provide a presence of prayer during the retreats that they were organizing there. These women, having raised their families, sought a way to deepen their spiritual lives. As early as 1930, they began to organize spiritual retreats. Geneviève Micheli, widowed after several years of happy marriage, was the anchor of this group from the start and continued her leadership even after she returned to Paris, the place of her birth.

Marguerite and Geneviève exchanged frequent letters from the late 1920s on. Following the death of Mother Geneviève in

December of 1961, Sister Marguerite prepared a collection of extracts from her correspondence with Mother Geneviève. The last of these, dated March 1944, was written from her chalet in the Upper Engadine. Geneviève had withdrawn there on one of the last trains to cross the frontier before the closure of the French border. Sister Marguerite had invited her to leave the comfort of this cherished retreat and to come to Grandchamp to serve as the leader of the nascent community. Geneviève struggled, just as Marguerite had done eight years earlier, to say "yes" to this call. In the end, her leadership was instrumental in the founding of the community.

It was as if Geneviève, like Father Couturier, had been prepared to listen attentively to the prompting of the Spirit. Immediately after her first meeting with him she knew how to communicate his vision of spiritual ecumenism in conversations with the sisters of the community, with retreatants, and with all those whom she met. Her father, a non-practicing Catholic, had married a Lutheran woman from Alsace. Geneviève married Leopold Micheli, who belonged to a Reformed family of Geneva. During her time in Paris, she took courses in spirituality at the Sorbonne, including one on Saint Bernard, while working to prepare the annual retreats. While in Paris she also encountered Pastor Wilfred Monod and joined the Protestant third order known as "Les Veilleurs,"[2] as did a number of the other women who later became sisters in the community.

During this period Geneviève had occasion to meet a number of significant figures from other churches, including Orthodox professors of theology Leon Zander and Paul Evdokimov. She was a close friend of Mother de Wavrechin, founder and prioress of the Benedictines of Sainte Françoise Romaine at Cormeilles-en-Parisis, where she often went for times of retreat.[3] She would have encountered Dom Lambert Beauduin, a pioneering leader of the liturgical renewal and founder of the Monastery of Unity at Chevetogne, during the years of "exile" that he spent there. It was in this very place, during vespers one evening, that Sister Marguerite experienced a call to community life. When Marguerite returned to Grandchamp from Paris, Irène Burnat was knocking at the door, wanting to join her and Sister Marthe (Marguerite Bossert), who was already living there to assist with the retreats. Pastor Jean de Saussure had proposed that Irène go to Grandchamp. And it was at his suggestion that Sister Marguerite asked to meet with Couturier while she was en route from the Protestant community of Pomeyrol where she had made an internship with the community, together with Irène. Pastor De Saussure knew Couturier well and became with him, co-president of the Protestant-Catholic dialogue known as the "Groupe des Dombes."[4] He would later serve as a chaplain to the community (1949-1954).

Mother Genviève was profoundly touched by Paul Couturier's positive reply to Marguerite's request for a meeting. She wrote, "I was deeply moved by Father Couturier's letter." She insisted, further, "yes, you must go; it is the response of God and you are working for his Reign and living this union that is a 'sign of new times' (...). I see possibilities and openings for you that come from the will of God. May you be truly open, and may you be humble and eager to respond. I carry you in my heart."[5] Several weeks later, she would write again to Sister Marguerite following her encounter with Couturier, "Your meeting with Father Couturier must have been truly wonderful. I wrote to him and he wrote back concerning the exceptionally profound "union" of minds, and of the importance of lived experience. I would like to have an opportunity to address this subject during the retreats, and to win others over to this idea."[6]

Sister Marguerite records her experience of the encounter with Couturier in her book, *Du grain à l'épi* (*From a Grain to the ear of wheat*): "On my return from Pomeyrol I stopped in Lyon for a day. I was welcomed by Father Couturier, and spent several hours with him. He confirmed me in my vocation to the common life and to pray for the unity of the church. (...) Soon after, three of us began living together."[7] Upon her return to Grandchamp, Sister Marguerite wrote to Couturier concerning their communion in prayer: "When we pray for the church, as we do every Saturday, think of us sometimes in the intercession for the church of Christ in Saturday evening prayer, and may He unite us all together in his love, a love that breaks down barriers. Thank you again for your kind hospitality."[8] This was the beginning of a deep bond of friendship. Father Couturier took to heart the invitation to carry the community in his prayer, often praying for the retreats held at Grandchamp, placing the programs on the altar as he celebrated Mass.

Geneviève Micheli traveled to Lyon to meet with Couturier soon after, in April 1940. Reporting at length to Marguerite on her return, she considered this a pivotal moment in her spiritual journey:

> My stopover in Lyon was one of the great days in my life and for my inner personal life, for the problems that have been heavy on my heart. It brought an extraordinary liberation or rather an admirable clarity concerning what love is in unity, and the adoration upon which unity must be founded. I think, love, and pray differently – you can thank God for that. And my heart has come to see Father Couturier, with Wilfred Monod, as my spiritual guides. Through this conversation I was given a great overview of the way to work for unity, and I came to see the retreat at Bièvres in a new spirit. I felt the Holy Spirit at work in a magnificent way (…) The pages that Father Couturier wrote for us on the phrase of the Lord's prayer, "Holy be your name," … gave the retreat a power and a depth that I have rarely felt, perhaps never to this degree. It is truly the dawning of a new era.[9]

Following the community's retreat of April 1940 on the theme, "Holy be your name," focused on Couturier's text, Sister Marguerite wrote to him to say that his reflection had made a deep impression upon them. It had inspired them to embrace a deep desire for the reconciliation of the churches, and a commitment to work and pray for unity. Recognizing the significance of this moment, she wrote, "I sense that we have taken a big step."[10]

Couturier was deeply encouraged by these first signs of the rebirth of monasticism within the Protestant churches. For some years he had been encouraging religious communities through his correspondence and his promotion of the Week of Prayer to pray without ceasing for unity. Through their spiritual bonds of prayer and real bonds of friendship he urged them to build up an "invisible monastery," a spiritual community united in prayer. Couturier's enthusiasm is reflected in his correspondence with Sister Marguerite. Following his first encounters with the sisters, he wrote, "May Grandchamp become a spiritual center of unionism. Remember, the only true method of unionism is the one based on spiritual realities, the method that one might call 'spiritual emulation.'"[11] He was heartened to learn, several months later, that they had embraced his vision and let it inform their life of prayer:

> To know that Grandchamp has become an *ardent* center of spiritual emulation, a center of prayer for that Christian unity that Christ asked of his Father ... God has called you to undertake the unionist task in the deepest sense. If he has called you to bring about a movement of contemplative life within Protestantism ... may he be blessed a thousand times! Visible unity is drawing near.[12]

For Couturier, Grandchamp represented a sort of visible incarnation of his dream for an invisible monastery of unity. In the fall of 1940 he confided to Geneviève, "I pray often for the 'invisible monastery,' of which Grandchamp is one of the most beautiful centers. I even get the feeling that the first *real* monastery of Christian unity as I understand it, will be Protestant."[13] His hopes were further confirmed when, the following year, the young Roger Schutz, a Swiss Reformed pastor and founder of the Taizé community, traveled to Lyon to meet Couturier and to share his desire to establish a small monastic community. After this meeting, Couturier wrote, "A part of what I dreamt of is coming to be! It is among my Protestant brethren that this real "monastery" is beginning, and I would also like to see it exist among Catholics."[14]

In March of 1941, the sisters wrote again to Father Couturier asking that he direct them to acquaintances of his experienced in the life of prayer who could lead a retreat focused on "an introduction to prayer." He sent them a collection of texts including one that he had penned himself, "A Cosmic Aspect of Prayer." It began, "breathing is the life of the body, prayer is the life of the soul," and concluded with the following exhortation: "When you pray, let my prayer become your prayer, become enriched by your prayer. Remember that I often stand like a beggar at the door of your soul." This is very much the tone that characterized his spirituality of prayer for unity, with its emphasis on praying to the Father with Christ for the unity that Christ desires. For Couturier, prayer for unity was always a matter of letting Christ's prayer for is disciples, "that all be one," dwell in us.

After the closure of the French border during the German occupation the grace of this intense exchange was no longer possible. Nonetheless, the bonds of spiritual friendship continued to be nourished through prayer. Father Geoffrey Curtis, an Anglican correspondent and biographer of Couturier would write of this period, "The Abbé's close friendship with the Protestant brothers of the Taizé community and with the Protestant sisterhood of Grandchamp ripened as darkness fell. It was to be of primary importance in their development and is still bearing fruit."[15]

In 1944 Geneviève Micheli became the leader of the community. From that time on she never ceased working to build up a monastic community and an extended community marked by a profound ecumenical openness. She did so by organizing meetings and lectures at Grandchamp, and through exchanges with Anglican, and later Roman Catholic religious communities. Contacts continued with the brothers of Taizé. During the years of the Second World War some of the first sisters would spend the winter months in Geneva where they joined the first brothers of Taizé for common prayer in the Cathedral. The bond between these two communities was strengthened following the war. In 1952 the first solemn professions took place, and the following year the sisters adopted the *Rule of Taizé*. The *Rule* contains an important exhortation to pray and work for unity: "Never resign yourself to the scandal of the separation of Christians, all so readily professing love for their neighbor, yet remaining divided. Make the unity of Christ's body your passionate concern."[16] Through the *Rule* Father Couturier's spiritual ecumenism continued to take root in the heart of the life of the Grandchamp community, even though, over time, the community may have lost sight of their debt to him for all that he had done to place them on this path. Today the sisters are reclaiming this rich heritage.

Through the years exchanges continued between the Sisters of Grandchamp and the brothers of Taizé, whose liturgical life[17] and teaching were often instructive for the sisters. From 1963 to 1990 sisters Marguerite and Gilberte lived at Taizé. Together with other sisters of Grandchamp they witnessed the inauguration of the Church of Reconciliation and shouldered the growing responsibilities of welcoming young pilgrims and guests. When, in 1969, some of the sisters were recalled to support the life of the motherhouse community at Grandchamp, the Sisters of Saint André assumed a greater share of the welcome at Taizé.

Today the Taizé community and its rule of life remain a vital touchstone for the ecumenical vocation of the Grandchamp community. Responding to their ecumenical calling, the sisters have lived out the practice of spiritual ecumenism through their presence at the Ecumenical Institute of Bossey, through their involvement in networks for reconciliation, justice, peace, and healing. More recently one of the sisters was named to the Protestant-Catholic dialogue founded by Paul Couturier, the Groupe des Dombes.

Brother Roger of Taizé once wrote, "A cry rises up from the suffering of humanity." He said, further, "The world needs exceptional persons who are known more for their attention to charity than for their natural qualities." Father Couturier was one of those exceptional beings, a holy man. His personality, his prophetic strength and humility are an inspiration. He gave his whole life for unity, right up to his dying breath, his whole being taken up more and more into the prayer of Christ, breathing only this prayer.

The Grace of a Monastic Vocation Today

In the uncertainty of today's world, women and men who are called to the grace of monastic life are, by virtue of their vocation, in a privileged situation. Having heard clearly God's "yes" to their lives, and responding by a "yes" that is given ever anew and more freely, they receive something like an interior foundation, a stability in God, a confidence. This foundation does not depend solely on the context of their vocation: the monastery, and sisters or brothers who are guided in their following of the rule by an abbess or abbot. These are indeed, part of the structure that supports them. Yet, today, many of these kinds of structures are weakening and breaking down. It is only to the extent that each monk is able to take charge of his or her own life, and become responsible for his or her personal life of faith and love and humanity, and co-responsible for the life of the monastery as a true bother or sister to others, that he or she will be able to withstand the pressures of life in the world, in the church, and in the monastery.

How is it that the monk might learn to take charge of his or her life and become responsible? This requires a period of monastic formation that includes instruction, and learning from the experience of a common life of prayer and work according to the spirit of the rule. Yet the most important agent of formation and inspiration is the Holy Spirit. The Spirit renews in us the love of Scripture through *lectio*, meditation, and the reading of the spiritual mothers and fathers of the church, both past and present. The Spirit is at work through the common life and daily work which is marked by the rhythm of common praise and culminates in the celebration of the eucharist.

Monastic life is a path towards greater freedom in obedience, producing a gradual transformation in a life of increasing simplicity and transparency. Crises, doubts, moments of rebellion and self-doubt are times of testing and opportunities to reaffirm that fundamental "yes" if we are able to open ourselves in trust to an elder or a guide who is there to listen and to welcome us in an attitude of prayer. The church and monastic life today have a particular need of monks, contemplative men and women who have learned from the Spirit to cry "Abba, Father!" (Romans 8: 15). Having learned to hear the Spirit crying out "Abba" in their hearts, they accept the reality of being beloved sons and daughters of God. From this deep awareness of their true belonging and existential relationship with the Father they can grow towards full spiritual maturity as authentically free children of God. In that same awareness they are enabled to say "yes" to the responsibility implied in their relationship with God, with others, and with all creation. They become genuine collaborators with God, partners in the covenant that the Father has made with his Son, the Lamb. They have learned to be docile to the Spirit, to listen, to obey, and assume their part in life with great simplicity, without abdicating their responsibilities.

All of creation and humanity is waiting, aspiring to meet men and women like these: free, responsible, open and compassionate to the extent that they take ownership of their own fragility, and woundedness. Such persons are aware of and assume their responsibility in solidarity with all of humanity and of creation. They are men and women of prayer and of compassion who know how to give of themselves when needed: salt that gives flavor, yeast that makes the bread of communion rise, a hearth of light that shines forth in hope.

Is the monk not destined to live "apart from all in order to be one with all"? The Holy Spirit helps us to grasp the dynamism contained in the saying of Evagrius. The Spirit ignites the fire of God's love in us so that our hearts might burn with the same love that dwelt in the heart of Jesus and that of Evagrius. The monk lives apart from others and sees the world as crucified. He or she is crucified for the world. His or her life is hidden with Christ in the Father, thought the Spirit. He or she is one with all people because the risen Christ, and through him the whole of humanity, dwells in their hearts.

The *oikumene* refers to the whole inhabited earth. God loves the world. God created it out of love and created human beings to share that love with them, so they in turn might care for God's creation. God sent his only Son to reveal that love to us, to help us believe in his unconditional love. The Father's desire is that all come to know and welcome his saving love and peace in Jesus, who is "the firstborn of a large family" (Romans 8:29). We are called to become brothers and sisters in Christ, as we allow ourselves to be gradually transformed into his image and likeness. The ecumenical vocation makes us aware of how important it is to be open to this transformation by the Spirit. Only then will we be "salt of the earth" and "light for the world" (Matthew 5:17).

Living in the spirit of the Beatitudes (Matthew 5:1-11), we strive to witness to the gospel through the quality of our common life, through attention and compassionate concern for all that goes on in the world, and solidarity with others. The Spirit makes our hearts burn with the desire for a world where all may dwell in peace, shalom, justice, and with respect for creation. Is not creation waiting "with eager longing for the revealing of the children of God?" (Romans 8:19)?

Some Aspects of Ecumenical Spirituality Lived by a Contemplative Community

The ecumenical vocation stands at the heart of the mystery of faith and in the prayer of Christ. Thus, its belongs at the center of ecclesial life, and must become a primary concern of all believers, and a principle "work" of each community that prays. The ecumenical calling is rooted in the death and resurrection of Christ. It has a global dimension, an openness to the universality of the Christian faith. It calls for a deep and humble spirit of repentance, an awareness of the attitudes of exclusion that have marked the Christian churches through the centuries, for example, regarding the Jewish people. It is the concern of every believer, yet it has been entrusted in a particular manner to consecrated men and women.

Through the Cross to a New Life in Communion

Before his passion, Jesus prayed to the Father for his disciples, "that they may all be one. As you, Father are in me, and I am in you, may they also be one in us so that the world may believe that you have sent me" (John 17:21). Giving of himself completely for others in order to reveal the Father's love, the sole aim of his mission (John 3:16), Jesus opened for us the path of love-communion, of unity. By laying down his life for his friends he showed us how to live (John 15:13). Through his self-giving love the forces of non-communion, of evil and death, were defeated. By his death on the cross, and in his unconditional acceptance of the Father's will to love, Jesus Christ gave us a new capacity to live in communion with one another. He prepared the way for us to pass from death to life, from fear to trust, from self-centeredness to openness, from self-justification to a humble turning to God, from sterility and inertia to the dynamic of the fullness of life.

No one can escape this passage through the way of the cross. It remains the only source of this radical newness of life that is love-communion. When confronted with the cross of Christ we become aware of our selfishness, our self-sufficiency, our desire for power, and of the feebleness of our good intentions (Matthew 16:23; Luke 22:33-34). The cross reminds us as well of the unconditional welcome of divine love: "Father, forgive them, for they do not know what they are doing" (Luke 23:34). The roots of all our divisions must be placed upon the cross to be crucified with him and buried with him in death (Galatians 5:24, 6:14; Romans 6: 4, 6). Baptism places us in this calling to openness and communion, to forgiveness and love in communion with Christ who has died and is risen. In our daily life we become aware of this calling and live it out and are gradually transformed as we begin each day anew in a life that is given over more and more to the Father, in a dynamic of self-giving which brings forgiveness, even of our enemies.

Christ entrusted the message of peace and forgiveness to his disciples. It is central to the message of the love of God, that

Good News to be handed on to all peoples. The only *raison d'être* for the church, the Body of Christ, is to live out and celebrate this forgiveness, to make it visible and tangible, following the example of Christ (John 13:34; 15:12; 20:21). The church is meant to be a sign of peace and unity, a seed of love and communion, a beacon of light in a suffering world (Philippians 2:15).

Participation in the Communion of the Divine Trinity

Those who welcome this new capacity and openness given by the Spirit are in tune with the deepest desire of the Father and the Son. Their life will be increasingly rooted in the life of the three divine persons, whose mutual sharing of life is an open communion. This mystery is admirably portrayed in Rublev's icon of the Trinity, known as the "Philoxenia," from the Greek word for the love of hospitality. The divine energy at work in the raising up of Jesus from the dead (Ephesians 1:19-21) can bring down the mountains of fear and hatred, the walls of separation and division that have been built up between peoples, and between the Christian confessions.

Through the gift of his Spirit, Christ entrusted this energy to his disciples, to his church, so that his work of life and healing might continue through them: "Peace be with you. As the Father has sent me, so I send you" (John 20:21). This power of the Spirit is not a possession or a privilege granted to a single community or to a particular church. When treated as such, it is rendered useless and powerless. There is nothing automatic or magical about the gift of the Spirit. It entails a weighty responsibility. In entrusting his mission of love, forgiveness, and peace to his disciples, Christ warns them not to bind up others in exercising the generosity of love which comes from the Father's heart, for the consequences will be great: "If you forgive the sins of any, they will be forgiven them; if you retain the sins of any, they are retained" (John 20:23). Jesus' words are an invitation to act with great care. The disciples can no longer act on their own strength and initiative, or to serve their own interests. Henceforth they act in his name, through the power of the Spirit. If they must take a stand, they can never claim to take the place of God, to be the only ones who are right, or to have full possession of the truth.

Through twenty centuries of the history of Christianity the sad reality of anathemas, excommunications, schisms, forced baptisms, the repression of cultures, and claims of cultural superiority have often hampered our ability to proclaim the Good News. The gift of forgiveness, the capacity to transcend ourselves, comes to us through the cross. It can only be received with a humble heart. Though others may resist the gift of reconciliation or fail to desire it, even to the point of breaking unity, it is not for us to consider them excluded from the grace and the faithfulness of God. The disciples of Christ are peacemakers, the humble of heart spoken of in the Beatitudes, seekers of the Spirit. Their life is no longer their own. Following the example of Christ (John 10:18), they lay it down for others, trusting all to the mercy of God.

The Unity of All Creation and the Ecumenical Vocation

The ecumenical vocation is inextricably bound up with the covenant of love that God has established with all creation (Genesis 8:21-22; 15; 17), with the people of Israel, and with the people of God, the church. We enter into this covenant relationship through baptism. Yet this very special and personal beginning does not diminish the universal character and goal of the Christian faith. Indeed, our relationship matures as we live in harmony with the loving plan of God the Father for all humanity, and for the entire cosmos.

The cornerstone of this vocation is Christ who has died and is risen. Grounded in him through baptism, our personal and communal life are nourished and renewed in the celebration of the Eucharist. In every aspect of the eucharistic celebration we see the love of God reaching out to every human person, no matter how far off they might be. Through the liturgy we are sensitized to hear the cries hidden deep within the reality of human suffer- ing and we are moved to prayers of intercession: "Lamb of God, you take away the sin of the world. Have mercy on us. Grant us peace." Through the mystery of baptism, which is completed and fully realized in the eucharist, we die with Christ. Everything that separates us from the Father, from others, from ourselves, is crucified and dies with him. Rising with him, we are reconciled with our deepest self, with all humanity, and with the whole of creation. With him, we become universal men and women.

Visitation: The Lived Experience of Communion

We often like to consider our lives as an ongoing experience of visitation. Mary and Elizabeth were women nourished by the Word of God. Their lives and their bodies were completely given over to the Word in expectation of the coming of the messiah. Like them, we experience how becoming progressively rooted in the mystery of faith, nourished by the Word, by prayer, and by the tender mercy of God, enables us to welcome with ever greater freedom the gifts that the Spirit desires to give us through others. Pope John Paul II recognized that the Spirit is at work in every person who prays, no matter what their background may be. The Church Fathers recognized the seeds of the Word at work beyond the frontiers of the church. Thus, our living out of the faith and our spirituality are greatly enriched through encounters with others. Such encounters also help us to clarify the heart of our Christian faith. We experience this grace of visitation in a special way through our encounters with several Catholic and Orthodox religious communities. Such exchanges lead us to a deeper prayer for the communion of the universal church within which this rich diversity will be welcomed and celebrated.

As a group of consecrated women we are particularly concerned and able to grasp deeply and respond to the ecumenical calling. In a life is rooted in prayer, our first task is to live out the love of God through our common life and with those around us. Following Christ in his poverty, chastity and obedience, we live with a simple spirit of openness to others, having no other motive than the glory of God and the salvation of the world. We cannot hide behind material or spiritual goods, and are called to receive all things in gratitude. Our open hands must be ever ready to bless and to share. Eager to share the gospel of peace, we offer the best of ourselves and seek out the best in others without fearing those who are different. We renounce all temptation to draw others to ourselves, or to our churches. Such a life is not without struggle, as the experience of Jesus shows. Often, the contemplative is called to withdraw in moments of solitude and prayer. Christ invites us to watch and pray with him at the foot of the cross. When the weight of the scandal of division becomes too heavy to bear, we are called to say "yes," to lay down our lives with Christ. At other moments the Spirit calls us to strike out on a journey towards others, as Mary went out to meet Elizabeth. We enjoy opportunities to gather with other women who, like Mary, are called to bear the Savior and bring him into the world. These are moments of visitation, times filled with joy and peace, with gratitude and praise for the treasure that they bear.

In the experience of visitation, as with any friendship, it doesn't take long for us to come up against differences. At Grandchamp this is part of the daily lot for sisters who come from different countries, cultures, denominational confessions, not to mention their different temperaments. The grace of visitation cannot grow and deepen without accepting the reality of the cross. Our communion in Christ enables us to become poor in spirit and to let go of any self-justification. In this way, the paschal mystery is at the heart of our life, and the eucharist, the culminating point of our prayer, remains the essential source of our communion with one another. This experience of being joined in a profound communion underlies our incessant prayer that our lived communion may one day be truly and freely expressed in the great thanksgiving meal of the eucharist. Christ left us the eucharist as a grace and a *viaticum*, a food for the journey in our spiritual combat to receive the love of God for ourselves and for the world.

Consecrated Women Called to a Vocation
of Prayer for Unity

Each day the Community of Grandchamp prays, "Lord, grant that Christians manifest the communion they share in you. May they all be one, so that the world may believe!" Communion is a gift entrusted to us so that we might live it in our communities and monasteries. Even our differences and weaknesses become like seeds of communion for our churches and for the world. In the past century, the experience of prayer for unity and efforts in favor of the rapprochement of the churches have helped us become more deeply aware of the scandal of separation within the Body of Christ. Doors have been opened and much progress was made. The hospitality and prayer of monastic communities has surely played an important role in these developments. Today we often hear tell of a "winter" of the ecumenical movement. At a structural level, this is certain. Within certain sectors of the Christian community there is a persistent fear of the "other," fear of change, a nostalgic wish to return to the past. Nonetheless, the hunger for unity is very much alive in the lives of many.

In future, it will be important for the churches to learn from and receive from one another's living traditions within the universal church. This is especially so for monastic communities where faith is called to descend into the heart, and theology becomes prayer, both personal and communal. Through encounter with others we come to understand "the breadth and length and height and depth" of the mystery of the love of Christ (Ephesians 3:18-19). There is much to discover in the lived experience of others that can lead us to the center, to the inexpressible love of God. Dorotheus of Gaza proposes the image of the wheel to consider how we are related to one another in Christ: "The more one approaches the center, the more we come closer to one another." Beneath different spiritual expressions we discover a fundamental unity in the experience of the love of God, in our common call to holiness. Metropolitan Eulogius once wrote, "The saints are citizens of the one universal church. They break down the walls of separation erected by

Christians who have not been faithful to the new commandment." The call to holiness is lived out in a particularly intentional way in the monastic life. Enzo Bianchi observes, "Monasticism is an abrupt path to holiness, a radical path of following Christ." It is a path of unity and oneness for each monk personally as well as for the brothers and sisters in their common life, and their life in the church and in the world.

Life in community is an opportunity to experience in microcosm the mystery of the universal church. Our life of common praise and intercession and the simplicity of our daily life in common are a humble reflection of the fellowship and communion that is at the heart of the church's vocation. We strive in all our humanity, and with the help of God's grace, to be of one heart and mind in Christ, whose ardent prayer and mission was that we might be truly reconciled so that the world may believe in his love.

Chapter Six

Baptists, Praying for Unity, and the Eschatology of Ecumenism

STEVEN R. HARMON

The title of this chapter will strike some readers as incongruous. The most striking incongruity may be its association of Baptists, long regarded by some observers as the problem children of the modern ecumenical movement, with a concern for Christian unity. Baptists have been quick to declare other traditions to be false churches. John Smyth, cofounder of the earliest identifiable Baptist congregation in Amsterdam in 1609, not only rejected his baptism in the Church of England as a false baptism; having concluded that no communion in Amsterdam, not even the believer-baptizing Mennonites with whom his group of English Separatist exiles had connections, was qualified as a true church to administer a true baptism, Smyth proceeded to baptize himself and the other members of his congregation.[1] Though Smyth soon regretted this action when he came to the conclusion that the Mennonites were indeed a true church and then sought to lead his congregation to be received into the Mennonite fellowship, his rebaptism foreshadowed the refusal of many of his present day ecclesiastical progeny to embrace the biblical and theological rationale for the mutual recognition of one baptism commended by *Baptism, Eucharist and Ministry*.[2] Baptists also have been quick to divide among themselves whenever some Baptists have become convinced that other Baptists have developed unbiblical patterns

of faith and practice. This happened in the earliest community
of Baptists in Amsterdam when a small group of its members led
by Thomas Helwys insisted on the validity of their baptisms as
administered by Smyth and in 1611 or 1612 returned to England
to establish Baptist ecclesial life in their homeland.[3] Baptists ever
since, especially in the United States, have tended to follow this fis-
siparous precedent for intra-Baptist relations in local congregations,
associations, national denominational organizations, and international Baptist bodies.[4] While the modern ecumenical movement
was anticipated by a proposal in 1806 by William Carey, a Baptist
missionary to India, that "a general association of all denominations of Christians from the four quarters of the earth" meet each
decade at the Cape of Good Hope,[5] Baptists have in the main tended
to be averse to the efforts of Faith and Order ecumenism toward
"visible unity in one faith and one eucharistic fellowship."[6] There
are significant exceptions to these generalizations about Baptists
and ecumenism.[7] Nevertheless, the attitudes of most Baptists to
ecumenism of the Faith and Order variety range from apathy to
outright antagonism.

A second incongruous combination in the title is ecumenism and eschatology. Some varieties of Christian eschatology have
fostered outright opposition to ecumenical alliances, while some
other forms of eschatology have been detrimental to robust ecumenical engagement in ways that are less obvious. The pessimism
of premillennialism did little to encourage hopes for any progress
toward visible Christian unity prior to the second advent of Christ
and his subsequent millennial kingdom, and dispensational premillennialism in particular branded the Roman Catholic Church as
"the whore of Babylon" and viewed the modern ecumenical movement as a precursor to a "one world church" supposedly foretold
in the Apocalypse. The historical optimism of postmillennialism
went hand in hand with the beginnings of the modern ecumenical
movement, but it also tended to make some ecumenically inclined
mainline Protestants impatient with church dividing doctrinal differences. When these have been regarded as unnecessary obstacles

to ecumenical advance that broad-minded modern (and now postmodern) Christians should easily be able to move beyond, the churches have tended to lose interest in the earnest contestation of differences of faith and order that must precede any lasting strides toward visible unity. While Eastern Orthodoxy and post-Vatican II Roman Catholicism are fully committed to the goals of Faith and Order ecumenism, from the perspective of Free Church Christians and many other Protestants these communions have fallen prey to an overly realized eschatology of the church that leads them to insist that other churches and ecclesiastical communities are deficient in aspects of faith and order while remaining insufficiently critical of the failures of their own churches.

Baptists have had their own share of entanglements with eschatologies that have not encouraged the healthiest ecumenical perspectives. While it is true that most early English Baptists distanced themselves from the millennarian fervor of the Fifth Monarchists[8] and that the most influential Baptist confessions in England and North America have offered simple affirmations of hope in the return of Christ that eschewed millennial speculation,[9] from the late nineteenth century onward Baptist churches and other Free Church communions have been fertile fields for the cultivation and propagation of dispensational premillennialism and thus also for its denunciation of ecumenism.[10] At the same time, many other non-dispensationalist Baptists nevertheless reacted strongly against the initiatives of the Faith and Order movement on account of a sort of Baptist triumphalism that paralleled the overly realized eschatologies of the church implicit in Catholic and Orthodox ecclesiology with similar, or perhaps worse, effects on Baptist attitudes toward other churches.[11] Yet at the core of the Baptist theological vision is a healthier sort of essential eschatological orientation that has the potential to help Baptists both to heed the dominical imperative of visible Christian unity and to offer their best gifts to the rest of the church through their participation in Faith and Order ecumenism. The remainder of this chapter will propose that the same eschatology inherent in the Baptist vision is the eschatology that is implicit in the act of praying for unity, an ecumenical endeavor that even Baptists who have reservations about Faith and Order ecumenism can embrace.

Just as there is no Christology or doctrine of the Trinity that is unique to Baptists, so also is there no distinctively Baptist eschatology. Yet Baptist theologian James Wm. McClendon, Jr. has persuasively contended that the baptist vision at its best is fundamentally eschatological. McClendon's three volume *Systematic Theology* is the most serious effort undertaken thus far to discern and articulate afresh the distinctiveness of the "baptist" vision, with the lower-case "b" spelling inclusive of Baptists proper and other Free Church communions from the sixteenth century Anabaptists to contemporary Pentecostal communities.[12] In the second volume titled *Doctrine* that addressed the question "what must the church teach to be the church now?," eschatology appears not at the end of the book but as the first rubric treated, and it is not so much as a separate doctrine as it is the key category "that can lead us to the whole of Christian doctrine."[13] The hermeneutical motto by which McClendon summarizes the baptist vision highlights its eschatological orientation: "this is that" and "then is now" – in other words, the story of the biblical people of God is the story of the present day community of faith, and the future disclosed in that story is to be embodied by the community now.[14]

The church's efforts to embody here and now the eschatological future disclosed in the biblical story ought to include the heeding of the dominical imperative of visible Christian unity. Two features of McClendon's treatment of the eschatology at the core of the baptist vision support this assertion. First, McClendon echoes and builds upon Paul Althaus in defining eschatology as the division of theology that is "about what lasts; it is also about what comes last, and about the history that leads from the one to the other."[15] Second, McClendon draws from Ludwig Wittgenstein in developing the eschatological introduction to *Doctrine* not in terms of a linear chronology of eschatological events but rather a series of interconnected "concrete end-pictures" suggested by the New Testament: the last judgment, the return of Jesus Christ, resurrection, death, hell, heaven, and the rule of God.[16] To these focal concrete end-pictures identified by McClendon we should add the visible unity of the followers of Christ, for that is precisely the concrete end-picture envisioned by Jesus in his prayer for those who believe in him in John 17. This is a perichoretic unity that participates in the life of the Triune God (vv. 11 and 21-23a), is in the process of being brought to full completion (v. 23b), and is a visible witness to the world of the love of God (v. 23c).[17] This prayer discloses a concrete end-picture in that it represents the eschatological hope of the person of God's self-disclosure. Such unity is therefore what lasts and what comes last, and its process of being brought to completion belongs to the history that leads from the one to the other. If McClendon has characterized the eschatological essence of the baptist vision rightly, and if the quest for the visible unity of the church rightly belongs to the fullness of this vision as John 17 suggests, then Baptists are being true to their historic ecclesial vocation when they devote themselves to the quest for visible unity in faith and order.

How might the eschatology of ecumenism implicit in Jesus' prayer in John 17 inform Baptist participation in this quest? The eschatology embedded in this prayer is that of the narrative sub-structure of the New Testament as a whole: the reign of God that has come near in Christ is already a present reality but is not yet fully realized.[18] The concrete end-picture of visible Christian unity partakes of this already-but-not-yet character of the reign of God. Christians already possess a unity that is Christological, in that they belong to the one body of Christ, and pneumatological, in that they are indwelt by one Spirit. But as the current divisions of the church attest, this unity is not yet fully realized, for its fullness is not visible. Indeed, to join Jesus in praying that believers may be one is to confess our current lack of unity. If unity, however, is conceived primarily as a spiritual reality, as Baptists have tended to do whenever they define the catholicity of the church in quantitative terms (i.e., as the universal church to which all Christians

belong),[19] then Baptists may see little reason to devote their energies to the earnest contestation of church dividing issues of faith
and order that must precede visible unity, for this christological
and pneumatological unity is already a present reality quite apart
from any visible manifestations of this unity. Likewise if visible
unity is only fully realized in the age to come, then there may be
little motivation to seek it in the present age. Not only Baptists but
many other Protestants have insisted that the four *notae ecclesiae*
of the Nicaeno-Constantinopolitan Creed, including the oneness
of the church, are *eschatological* marks of the church. This is true
enough, but one legacy of this insistence is an aversion to efforts
to realize these marks, especially the mark of visible oneness, in
the present. If the oneness, holiness, catholicity, and apostolicity
of the church will fully be realized only eschatologically, that does
not mean that the church should not seek to attain to those marks
in the present.

The inadequacy of both of these patterns of relating eschatology to the ecumenical task is apparent in light of an analogous
relation of eschatology to the saints' quest for holiness of life. Even
now in this earthly life, the saints already are just that – "holy ones"
(Ephesians 1:1) who are "seated with him in the heavenly places
in Christ Jesus" (Ephesians 2:6 NRSV). But in this earthly life the
saints are not yet fully holy in person or practice. The completion
of sanctification awaits the "eternal weight of glory beyond all
measure" (2 Corinthians 4:17), even if one grants the possibility
of "entire sanctification" according to Wesleyan theology or of
the earthly realization of divinization in the Orthodox tradition.
Just as the present positional holiness of the saints in Christ does
not warrant a refusal of the sanctifying work of the Spirit in the
present, and just as the deferral of the glorification of the saints
until the resurrection should not de-motivate the present pursuit
of the sanctification that will be completed in the eschaton, so
with the already/not-yet nature of Christian unity. It is precisely
because the church has already been entrusted with the lasting
reality of oneness in Christ and in the Spirit that the church must

seek to make this oneness visible to the world in advance of the age to come, and it is precisely because visible unity is a concrete end-picture disclosed by Jesus himself that the church can be confident that she is joining God in what God intends to do in and through the church in the culmination of God's goals for all things when she participates in the kind of quest for visible unity that is envisioned by the New Delhi statement on the goals of Faith and Order ecumenism:

> We believe that the unity which is both God's will and God's gift to God's church is being made visible as all in each place who are baptized into Jesus Christ and confess him as Lord and Saviour are brought by the Holy Spirit into one fully committed fellowship, holding the one apostolic faith, preaching the one gospel, breaking the one bread, joining in common prayer, and having a corporate life reaching out in witness and service to all who at the same time are united with the whole Christian fellowship in all places and all ages in such wise that ministry and members are accepted by all, and that all can act and speak together as occasion requires for the tasks to which God calls God's people.[20]

Like the baptist vision at its best, Faith and Order ecumenism at its best is concerned with what lasts, what comes last, and the history that leads from the one to the other.

Whenever Baptists observe the Week of Prayer for Christian Unity (and many Baptist congregations do so) or engage in other forms of corporate and individual prayer in which they join their Lord in praying for the visible unity of his church, they embody these connections between the Baptist vision, eschatology, and ecumenism. Theological reflection on Baptist practices of praying for Christian unity suggests the following four observations regarding the significance of such acts in light of the foregoing claims about the eschatology of ecumenism.

First, praying for Christian unity moves Baptists to confess as sin their own contributions to division in the body of Christ. To ask God to grant unity to the church is to admit that the church does not yet have the unity God intends, and the appropriate first response to this admission for any Christian communion is to ask, "Is it I, Lord?" All churches have their own particular sins against the unity of the church to confess, and Baptists are certainly no exception. Prayer for Christian unity exposes the sinfulness of the energies Baptists have devoted to their own internal divisions, of their preoccupation with preserving Baptist distinctiveness while neglecting to form the faithful in Christian essentials, of failing to recognize the one who is the Truth in the faith and practice of non-Baptist churches with which they disagree, and of all manner of other transgressions against the unity of the body of Christ known only by the Spirit in whom they offer prayer for Christian unity.

Second, praying for Christian unity reminds Baptists of the distinctive gifts they have to offer to the larger body of Christ through their participation in the quest for visible unity. If asking God to grant unity to the church involves an admission that the church is not yet unified, this admission may also lead to the humble identification of the legitimate points of dissent that are involved in the present divisions and that must be maintained until mutual ecclesial conversion to the church's Lord makes possible closer convergences of faith and practice. The eschatological character of the Baptist vision makes Baptists wary of identifying any earthly institution with the full realization of the unity for which Christ prayed. This aversion to overly realized eschatologies of the church is manifest in what Baptist theologian Nigel Wright has called "the disavowal of Constantine," by which he means the Baptist witness against symbiotic patterns of relationships between the church and the civil power that have resulted in the compromise of the church's counter-cultural stance vis-à-vis the powers that be and that have sometimes resulted in the civil power's coercion of the church to do the bidding of the state.[21] Even if the Roman Catholic Church is irrevocably committed to the principle of religious liberty by the Vatican II Declaration on Religious Liberty (*Dignitatis Humanae*),[22] and even though the church has become legally and/or culturally disestablished in much of the Western world, Baptists have their origin in dissent from church corrupting relationships between church and state, and they still have this witness to offer to the rest of the church – and to themselves, inasmuch as Baptists too have sometimes fallen prey to the temptations of Christendom. Baptists have also rightly dissented from the wielding within the church of what Wright calls "sacred power," by means of which ecclesiastical hierarchies have sometimes coerced the faithful.[23] Inasmuch as there are forms of church life that do not easily admit themselves to correction by a radical application of the Vincentian criterion of consent by the faithful (*ab omnibus creditum est* – "that which has been believed *by all*") for discerning that which is truly authoritative in the teaching of the church, [24] therefore also embodying an overly realized eschatology of the church which does not reckon seriously enough with its not-yet-perfected character, Baptists continue to insist that those dimensions of ecclesiology are church dividing and must be earnestly contested before visible unity is possible. Praying for unity can help Baptists contribute to the quest for visible unity by steering them, however indirectly, toward reclaiming their ecclesial vocation as dissenting catholics even while fostering humility in the practice of their dissent.[25]

Third, praying for Christian unity embodies the Baptist emphasis on the priesthood of all believers by inviting all members of the church to participate actively in the foundational ecumenical practice upon which all other forms of ecumenical engagement depend. The concept of the priesthood of all believers is not unique to Baptists. It is after all a biblical concept (1 Peter 2:9), and though the Protestant Reformers of the sixteenth century emphasized it, the universal priestly ministry of believers is taught in the *Catechism of the Catholic Church*.[26] Baptists have nevertheless lent to the priesthood of believers an emphasis on the responsibility of all members of the congregation to do the ministry of the local church in accordance with congregational polity. Applied to the quest for the visible unity of the church, the cherished Baptist principle of the priesthood of all believers means that heeding the ecumenical imperative is the task not only of theologians and ecumenists, and not only of the pastors whose office should entail maintaining the unity of the church in an ecclesiology that equates the biblical offices of bishop and pastor, but also of the laity. Laypersons are the ones who truly embody the quest for Christian unity in their relationships with other Christians who belong to other communions, and it is most appropriate that they constitute the majority of those who are called to prayer during the Week of Prayer for Christian Unity and at other times when the church follows the lead of her Lord in praying "that they may all be one."[27] Given the resistance of many Baptists to Faith and Order initiatives that they regard as "organic union schemes," the practice of praying for unity may also be the most appropriate way for most Baptists to begin participating in the one ecumenical movement – and it is the ecumenical practice that is most crucial for the success of the movement, if indeed we believe with the authors of the New Delhi report that "unity is God's gift to God's church."[28]

Fourth, praying for Christian unity provides Baptists and other Christians with a proper perspective on their participation in the quest for visible Christian unity. Praying for unity reminds the church that unity is God's gift: it comes about as the divided churches are converted to Christ by the work of the Holy Spirit in their midst, not through the human efforts of the church to bring about its own unity. Furthermore, if such prayer is oriented toward what lasts, what comes last, and the history that leads from the one to the other, then what is sought by those who pray for unity may not be granted during their earthly lives. The already-inaugurated-but-not-fully-realized character of the reign of God presupposed by such prayer is a proper motivation for the rigorous but patient contributions of theologians, ecumenists, and all members of their churches to the ecumenical goal of "one eucharistic fellowship," a goal that in all likelihood will not be realized in their lifetimes and indeed may require centuries of ecclesial commitment to the contestation of faith and order apart from unforeseen actions of the Spirit that may yet initiate long awaited eschatological emergences. Praying for unity keeps the church from losing heart in what increasingly seems, from a human point of view, to be a losing struggle.

The past two years have not been encouraging to those who hope, pray, and work for Christian unity. In February 2006 the Foundation for a Conference on Faith and Order in North America agreed to dissolve itself after plans to host in 2005 a more broadly inclusive sequel to the original North American Conference on Faith and Order that had been held in Oberlin, Ohio in 1957 failed to materialize.[29] On July 10, 2007, the Vatican released a June 29 document from the Congregation for the Doctrine of the Faith offering "Responses to Some Questions Regarding Certain Aspects of the Doctrine of the Church."[30] Even though this document clearly reiterated what the Vatican II Decree on Ecumenism (*Unitatis Redintegratio*) and John Paul II's papal encyclical *Ut Unum Sint* generously affirmed regarding the presence of Christ and the work of the Spirit in other churches and ecclesial communities that are separated from the Roman Catholic Church,[31] media mischaracterizations of the document contributed to worldwide outrage at what many regarded as a major step away from the Rome's post-Vatican II commitments to ecumenical engagement.

At the beginning and end of 2006, I participated in conferences with varying degrees of indirect relation to the events mentioned in the preceding paragraph. In January 2006 I was a member of a consultation convened by the Foundation for a Conference on Faith and Order in North America that met for three days at the Graymoor Ecumenical and Interreligious Institute in Garrison, New York primarily to examine the factors behind the failure of the envisioned Second Conference on Faith and Order in North America, but secondarily to contemplate the possibilities for such a conference in the future. While some of the presentations and discussions evidenced a remarkable degree of ecumenical energy among the constituencies represented at the consultation, the gathering seemed like a funeral for the death of an ecumenical dream. And yet when we joined in common worship each morning and evening, singing Taizé chants and praying together for the unity of the church, we experienced the rekindling of a hope that did not seem warranted by the circumstances. In December 2006 I served as a member of the Baptist World Alliance delegation to the first round of a new five year series of conversations with the Pontifical Council for Promoting Christian Unity that met at Beeson Divinity School, an interdenominational evangelical divinity school at Baptist related Samford University in Birmingham, Alabama. In contrast to the Graymoor consultation, the mood of these conversations was far from somber; yet all participants were acutely aware of the inevitable ecclesiological impasses that lay ahead. Even so, when the delegates gathered for morning and evening prayer each day in Beeson's Andrew Gerow Hodges Chapel, where Thomas Aquinas and Martin Luther significantly stand side-by-side facing worshipers among the sixteen representatives of the communion of saints whose frescoes encircle the chapel's dome, those who were not yet able to be united at the Lord's table were nevertheless able to be united in praying together along with their Lord that they might one day be made one. Both of these experiences of praying for unity at the boundaries of the church's divisions underscore the eschatology of ecumenism that makes this a most appropriate grassroots ecumenical practice for Baptists – and for all other Christians.

My own hope is that in some unforeseen way, Baptists might one day come to have the same function in one visibly united church that our pre-Reformation predecessors as "believers' churches," namely the communities and orders that emerged from the patristic and medieval renewal movements of monasticism, have had as committed fellowships that call the one church to renewal from within. While we remain separated ecclesial communities in the not-yet-realized aspect of the church's eschatology, we can join those from whom we are otherwise separated in the common labor of praying for unity.

Notes

Introduction

1   In *The Apostolic Fathers*. Kirsopp Lake, trans. (Cambridge: Harvard UP, 1985; Original edition: London: W. Heinneman, 1912).

2   John Paul II, *Ut Unum Sint. On Commitment to Ecumenism* (Washington, DC: USCCB Publications, 1995), par. 29.

3   Walter Kasper, *Handbook of Spiritual Ecumenism* (New York: New City, 2007).

4   *Ut Unum Sint*, par. 28.

5   See Charles LaFontaine, *'Repairer of the Breach': Mother Lurana White, Co-Founder of the Society of the Atonement* (Graymoor, 1976); Mary Celine, *A Woman of Unity: Mother Lurana of Graymoor* (Graymoor: Franciscan Society of the Atonement, 1956).

6   *Franciscan Friars and Sisters of the Atonement Centennial. Society of the Atonement 1898-1998: Ut omnes unum sint: Commentary, Celebrating, Continuing* (Graymoor: Franciscan Friars of the Atonement, 1997).

7   For more on Paul Wattson, see David Gannon, *Father Paul of Graymoor* (New York: MacMillan, 1951); Titus Cranny, *Paul Wattson: Apostle of Unity* (Peeksgill: Graymoor Press, 1955; Second edition, 1965); Titus Cranny, ed., *The Words of Father Paul*. 16 vols. (Garrison, NY: Graymoor, 1952); Titus Cranny, ed., *Father Paul and Christian Unity: An Anthology on Christian Reunion Prepared from the Writings, Sermons and Addresses of Father Paul James Francis, s.a. (1863-1948)* (Peeksgill: Graymoor, 1963); Charles Angell and Charles LaFontaine, *Prophet of Reunion: The Life of Paul of Graymoor* (New York: Seabury, 1975).

8   The standard English language biography of Couturier was written by Geoffrey Curtis, of the Anglican Community of the Resurrection. Curtis was a frequent correspondent and collaborator in the promotion of the Week of Prayer. See *Paul Couturier and Unity in Christ* (London: SCM Press, 1964).

Chapter Two

1   See Thomas Aquinas, *Summa Theologica*, IIa, IIae, q. 83, a. 1.

2   See Yves Congar, *Jésus-Christ: notre médiateur, notre Seigneur* (Paris: Cerf, 1965), p. 84.

3   John's Gospel underscores this fact. See for example, John 5:44; 7:18; 8:54.

4   See the issues that have once again been raised in the statement of the Congregation of the Doctrine of the Faith, "Responses to Some Questions Regarding Certain Aspects of the Doctrine on the Church," (July 10, 2007) concerning the extension of the word church to other ecclesial communities. In *Origins* 37, no. 9 (July 19, 2007): 134-136.

5   UR 8.

6   See Yves Congar, "Les ruptures de l'unité," *Istina* 10, nos. 2-3 (1964): 164f.

7   Some of these who were influenced by a renewal movement begun in Scotland in the 1740's including Jonathan Edwards (1705-1758) and James Stewart who wrote the influential *Hints for a General Union of Christians for Prayer for the Outpouring of the Holy Spirit*. The ideas contained in this work would later bear fruit in the Evangelical Alliance's Week of Prayer begun in 1846 whose purpose was to have Christians pray for the outpouring of the Spirit for revival and renewal during the first calendar week of each year. For this information, see the work of R. Mercer, *What is this 'Week of Prayer for Christian Unity'?* (London: SPCK / CTS, [1977]), pp. 2f.

8   R.F. Esposito, *Leone XIII e l'Oriente Cristiano* (Rome: Ed. Paoline, 1960), p. 457. For commentary on these texts see also C. Boyer & D. Bellucci, eds., *Unità cristiana e movimento ecumenico* (Rome: Studium, 1963), pp. 31 ff.

9   In a quote from David Gannon, *Father Paul of Graymoor* (New York: Macmillian, 1951), p. 260: we learn that Wattson related the choice of the dates for his Octave to some theological concepts when he explained why he proposed eight days for prayer for unity rather than just one: "The fitness of an Octave beginning with a festival in honor of what God himself has constituted the Centre of Catholic Unity, viz., The Chair of Peter, and ending with the feast of the Conversion of the great Apostle to the Gentiles (...). When the Founder of Christianity prayed for the Unity of His disciples, the reason He gave was 'That the world might believe.' We are, therefore, to begin with Unity that we may end in the Conversion of the whole of world – The Chair of Peter stands for the first; St. Paul, the missionary convert, stands for the latter."

10   Information from the archives of the Faith and Order Commission cited by D. Heller, "The Soul of the Ecumenical Movement. The History and Significance of the Week of Prayer for Christian Unity," *The Ecumenical Review* 50, no. 3 (1998): 404, n. 5. See also the special issue of the *Ecumenical Review*: 100 Years of the Week of Prayer for Christian Unity, 59, no. 4 (2007).

11   *AAS* 9, no. 2 (1917): 61F.

12   It should be noted that in 1949 the Sacred Congregation of the Holy Office issued *Ecclesia Catholica*, "Instruction to Local Ordinaries on the Ecumenical Movement" that attributed the movement toward unity to be the work of the Holy Spirit. It will be another decade and a half before the Catholic Church officially enters the ecumenical movement at the Second Vatican Council.

13   *LG* 15.

14   In his letter *Equidem Verba* of March 21, 1924, Pope Pius XI encouraged the Benedictines to pray for Christian unity which led to the founding of the monastery at Amay-sur-Meuse in 1925 which moved to Chevetogne in 1939. Their purpose was to help establish relations between Catholics and Orthodox. In addition there are Benedictines who are members of the Anglican Communion just as there are Franciscans who are Anglicans.

15   See M. Woodruff, "Paul Couturier, the Week of Prayer, and the Unity of Humanity in Christ," in M. Woodruff, ed., *The Unity of Christians: The Vision of Paul Couturier* (Oxford: The Catholic League, 2005), pp. 141f.

16   For all the themes through 2008, see appendix.

17   *Cf.* "Prayer for Unity, The Report of the Consultation on 'The Future of the Week of Prayer for Christian Unity', Geneva, October 1966," *One in Christ* 3, no. 3 (1967): 251-261.

18   Pontifical Council for Promoting Christian Unity, *Directory for the Application of Principles and Norms on Ecumenism* (Washington, DC: USCCB Publications, 1993), par. 63.

19   John Paul II, *Ut Unum Sint. On Commitment to Ecumenism* (Washington, DC: USCCB Publications, 1995), par. 26. On the many experiences of ecumenical prayer celebrated by the Bishop of Rome, see G. Viviani, "The Ecumenical Liturgies Celebrated by the Holy Father in Rome and in the World: 'The Common Prayer with our Brothers and Sisters who Seek Unity in Christ and in His Church' (*Ut Unum Sint*, 24)," in J.F. Puglisi, ed., *Liturgical Renewal as a Way to Christian Unity* (Collegeville: Liturgical Press, 2005), pp. 147-198.

20   For example, see the issues raised by the Congregation for the Doctrine of the Faith, "Responses to Some Questions Regarding Certain Aspects of the Doctrine on the Church," issued 10 July 2007. Reaction and explanation of this text was immediate which shows how sensitive the issues are. For example, see

the commentary of J. Wicks, "Questions and Answers on the New *Responses of the Congregation for the Doctrine of the Faith*" *Ecumenical Trends* 36, no. 7 (2007): 1/97-7/103, 15/111-16/112 which places this text in the context of other more important magisterial texts (Council Decrees and Encyclicals) as well as lower level texts issued by Dicasteries of the Holy See. One of the central points revolves around the definition of the Catholic Church in relation to the Church of Christ. This section of the document needs to be read together with the comments previously made by Cardinal Jan Willebrands, "Vatican II's Ecclesiology of Communion," *Origins* 17, no. 2 (1987): 27-33 and *One in Christ* 23, no. 3 (1987); and F. Sullivan, "'Subsistit in': The Significance of Vatican II's Decision to Say of the Church of Christ not that it 'is' but that it 'subsists in' the Roman Catholic Church," *One in Christ* 22, no. 2 (1986): 115-123.

21   See, John Paul II, *Ut Unum Sint*, par. 78.

22   Cited by T. Cranny, *John 17: As We are One* (Peekskill, NY: Graymoor Press, 1965), p. 90.

Chapter Three

1   For a general account of the history of the Church of England, see J. R. H. Moorman, *A History of the Church in England* (London: A&C Black, Third Edition, 1973). The wider picture is surveyed in Stephen Neill, *Anglicanism* (Harmondsworth: Penguin, 1958): his perspective is valuable because he wrote before the post-1960s assumption that the Anglican tradition has always been "inclusive" and "ecumenical."

2   See most recently G. E. Bernard, *The King's Reformation: Henry VIII and the Remaking of the English Church* (New Haven: Yale, 2005).

3   Prayer for the Church, 1549 Holy Communion service: this remains unchanged in all successive revisions – 1552 (Edward VI), 1559 (Elizabeth), 1604 (James I) and 1662 (Charles II). The 1637 *Book of Common Prayer* (Charles I), whose contents were a contributing factor to the civil war, was taken up in the Episcopal Church of Scotland but not in the Church of England: as regards prayer for unity it does not differ from the 1662 *Book of Common Prayer*.

Citations from Reformation era prayer books are taken from Joseph Kelly, ed., *The Two Liturgies, AD 1549 and AD 1552, with other Documents set forth by Authority in the Reign of King Edward VI* (Cambridge: The University Press, for the Parker Society, 1844), and Wm. Keating, ed., *Liturgies and Occasional Forms of Prayer Set Forth in the Reign of Queen Elizabeth* (Cambridge: The University Press, for the Parker Society, 1847).

4   Further evidence that church life was less than smooth can be seen in prayers published in Edward VI's Primer (1553, the year of his death, after which the book was withdrawn). The prayer, "Of all Christians" notes that "as all the members of a body have not one office," God is asked to send "the spirit of love with concord among us, that without any disorder or debate every one of us may be content with our calling."

5   See W. B. Patterson, *King James VI and I and the Reunion of Christendom* (Cambridge: Cambridge UP, 1997).

6   The Preface also notes the need for a service of "Baptism for such as are of Riper Years," both because of the "growth of Anabaptism, through the licentiousness of the late times crept in amongst us" and also "may be always useful for the baptizing of Natives in our Plantations, and others converted to the Faith." This presages the trade and colonial expansion which would lead to the British Empire, and, alongside missionary work, the emergence of a global network of churches derived from the Church of England, the Anglican Communion.

7   The Accession Service was appended by Royal Warrant of Charles II, omitted by William and Mary, appended again by Anne, including the new Prayer for Unity, and retained until 1859, when the service was withdrawn finally by Royal Warrant.

8   Ruth Rouse & Stephen Neill, eds., *A History of the Ecumenical Movement*. Second Edition (London: SPCK, 1967), p. 315. Part of Chapter 7, "Voluntary Movements and the Changing Ecumenical Climate" by Ruth Rouse. Chapter 3, "Ecumenical Movements in Great Britain in the 17th and 18th Centuries," by Norman Sykes, sets out the fuller background to this paragraph.

9   Rouse, "Voluntary Movements," p. 345.

10   For an overview of the Australian situation, see Muriel Porter, *Land of the Spirit?* (Geneva: WCC, 1990), and Ian Breward, *'The Most Godless Place Under Heaven?'* (Melbourne: Beacon Hill, 1988).

11   Rouse, "Voluntary Movements," pp. 320-321; see also Don Herbert Yoder, "Christian Unity in Nineteenth-century America," in *A History of the Ecumenical Movement*, pp. 254-256. The choice of the week following the first Sunday of the civil year may arise from John Wesley's institution of a Covenant service for "the people called Methodist" on that Sunday.

12   Rouse, "Voluntary Movements," pp. 345-346.

13   The prayer echoes the prayers associated with the Peace in the Latin rite. An initial papal blessing for the Association changed to an in principle condemnation in 1864, and Roman Catholic members had to withdraw. See Rouse, "Voluntary Movements," p. 347.

14   See Randall Davidson, ed., *The Lambeth Conferences of 1867, 1878 and 1898, with the Official Reports and Resolutions, Together with the Sermons Preached at the Conferences* (London: SPCK, 1889), p. 332.

15   Davidson, *The Lambeth Conferences*, pp. 15 and 97. The original draft did not contain the citation of John 17:21-22 and the following "maintaining the faith" reason. Its strengthening shows that the deliberations of the bishops moved them to place greater emphasis on unity beyond the immediate situation which faced them.

16   Davidson, *The Lambeth Conferences*, pp. 81-82.

17   Davidson, *The Lambeth Conferences*, p. 89. Stern warnings about developments in the Roman Catholic Church condition the scope of the unity envisaged: the 1867 "Address to the Faithful" states, "We entreat you to guard yourselves against the growing superstitions and additions with which in these latter days the truth of God hath been overlaid; as otherwise, so especially by the pretension to universal sovereignty over God's heritage asserted by the See of Rome, and by the practical exaltation of the Blessed Virgin Mary as mediator in place of her Divine Son, and by the addressing of prayers to her as intercessor between God and man. Of such beware, we beseech you, knowing that the jealous God giveth not His honour to another."

18   Davidson, *The Lambeth Conferences*, pp. 169-170.

19   The Conference also addressed the 1870 pronunciation of the Bishop of Rome being able to make infallible statements in terms even sterner than those of 1867: "an invasion of the attributes of the Lord Jesus Christ." Davidson, *The Lambeth Conferences*, p. 182.

20   Rouse, "Voluntary Movements," p. 340.

21   The Conference "Encyclical Letter" summarizes these points: in each case negative reference is made to "Roman Catholic brethren" with whom "under the present conditions [i.e. the (First) Vatican Council], it was useless to consider the question of Reunion." See Davidson, *The Lambeth Conferences*, pp. 264-276 and 335.

22   *Conference of Bishops of the Anglican Communion Holden at Lambeth Palace in July 1897* (London: SPCK, 1897), pp. 25-6, 42.

23   See *The Lambeth Conference 1930. Encyclical Letter from the Bishops with Resolutions and Reports* (London: SPCK, 1930), pp. 110-120; Rouse, "Voluntary Movements," pp. 347-348; Stephen Neill, "Plans for Union and Reunion, 1917-1948," in Neill & Rouse, eds., *History of the Ecumenical Movement*, pp. 447-448. Copies of the Appeal were sent officially to the Pope, Eastern patriarchs and English Dissenters.

24   Lambeth 1930 took up "The Unity of the Church" as a major topic, responding in particular to the 1927 Faith and Order Conference, as did Lambeth 1948, supporting the formation of the World Council of Churches. Both Conferences devoted considerable energy to issues related to the formation of the Church of South India, but neither say anything in particular about prayer for unity, or the now established Week of Prayer for Christian Unity.

25   Though the latter book was not legalized by parliament, its non-controversial sections, including these two prayers for unity, were quickly taken up across the Communion.

26   Rouse, "Voluntary Movements," p. 348.

27   Ibid.

28   The most recent ARCIC Agreed Statement, *Mary: Grace and Hope in Christ* (London: Morehouse, 2005) takes up the issue of intercession in particular.

Chapter Four

1   Helene Iswolsky, *No Time to Grieve. An Autobiographical Journey* (Philadelphia: The Winchell Company, 1985), pp. 257-258.

2   Edward Hanahoe, *Two Early Documents on Reunion* (Graymoor, NY: National Office, Chair of Unity Octave, 1954).

3   These contacts are described in Maurice Villain's autobiography, *Vers l'Unité. Itinéraire d'un Pionnier. 1935-1975* (Paris: G.S.O.E., 1986), pp. 141-148.

4   Kenneth Hagen, *Luther's Approach to Scripture as Seen in his "Commentaries" on Galatians. 1519-1538* (Tübingen: J. C. B. Mohr, 1993), p. vii.

5   *Theologia dogmatica christianorum orientalium ab Ecclesia catholica dissidentium* (Paris: Letouzey et Ané, 1926-35); *La Mort et l'Assomption de la Sainte Vierge. Etude historico-doctrinale* (Città del Vaticano: Biblioteca apostolica vaticana, 1944).

6   *Equidem verba*, a 1924 letter to the Prior of the Benedictine monastery of Amay (the presentday community at Chevetogne).

7   Motu propio *Superno Dei Nutu*, 5-6 1960, in *Acta et Documenta Concilio Oecumenico Vatican II apparando, Series I*, vol. I (Typis Polyglottis Vaticanis 1960), p. 93.

8   There is an Italian book by Mario Sensi on the contribution made to Vatican Council II by the historians of the Lateran University; I have been unable to find it. [This is likely a reference to: Mario Sensi, "Monsignor Michele Maccarone et l'apporto della scuolo storia Lateranense al Vaticano II," *Centro Vaticano* V, I. Editor]

9   *La Théologie Oecuménique. Notion - Formes - Démarches* (Louvain: Warny, 1960); *Histoire Doctrinale du Mouvement Oecuménique* (Paris: Desclée, 1962).

10   Antoine Wenger, *Vatican II. Chronique de la Deuxième Session* (Paris: Le Centurion, 1964), pp. 200-201; Wenger, the religious redactor of the French daily, *La Croix*, was the only journalist authorized to attend the sessions of the council. He did not attend the meetings of the conciliar commissions.

11   I have deposited the original of this letter in the Weigel Archives at Georgetown University.

12   Patrick W. Collins, *Gustave Weigel. A Pioneer of Reform* (Collegeville: Litugical Press, 1991), pp.178-179.

13   "Praying together: *Communicatio in sacris* in the Decree on Ecumenism," in Alberic Stacpoole, ed., *Vatican II by Those Who Were There* (London: Geoffrey Chapman, 1986), pp. 202-219.

14   The passage is in article 7: *De culpis adversus unitatem valet testimonium S. Joannis: "Si dixerimus quoniam non peccavimus: mendacem facimus eum, et verbum ejus non est in nobis" (1 Jo 1 :10). Humili igitur prece veniam petimus a Deo et a fratribus sejunctis, sicut et nos dimittimus debitoribus nostris.* ["The words of St. John hold good about sins against unity : 'If we say we have not sinned, we make him a liar, and his word is not in us' (1 Jn 1:10). So we humbly beg pardon of God and of our separated sisters and brothers, just as we forgive all them who trespass against us." Cf. "Decree on Ecumenism," in *Decree of the Ecumenical Councils*, vol. II, ed. Norman P. Tanner, (Georgegtown: Georgetown UP / London: Sheed & Ward, 1990), p. 913.]

15   This text is in article 23: *Quod si inter Christianos multi not semper eadem ratione atque Catholici Evangelium de re morali intelligunt neque easdem solutiones difficiliorum hodiernae societatis quaestionum admittunt, nihilominus ut nos volunt Verbo Christo ut fonti christianae virtutis haerere et apostolico obedire praecepto: "Omne quodcumque facitis in verbo aut in opere, omnia in nomine Domini Jesu Christi, gratias agentes Deo et Patri per Ipsum" (Col. 3 :17). Hinc dialogus oecumenicus de morali Evangelii applicatione initium sumere potest.* ["While it is true that some other Christians do not always understand the moral teaching of the gospel in the same way as Catholics, and do not accept the same solutions to the more difficult problems of modern society, nevertheless they share our desire to stand by (Christ the Word) as the source of Christian virtue, and to obey the command of the apostle: 'Whatever you do, in word or in work, do all in the name of the Lord Jesus, giving thanks to God the Father through him' (Col 3:17)." Cf. "Decree on Ecumenism," in Tanner, p. 920. (This translation also has "Christ's word." Editor)] Walter Abbott's *The Documents of Vatican II* (New York: Guild Press, 1966), p. 365, translates *Verbo Christo* as though it were *verbo Christi*: "Christ's word," intead of "Christ the Word"; another version also says, "Christ's word"

(*The Decree on Ecumenism*, [Glen Rock, NJ: Paulist Press, 1965], p. 81); Austin Flannery's *The Documents of Vatican II* (New York: Pillar Books, 1975), p.470, has: "the word of Christ." In good theology it is not "the word of Christ" that is the source of Christian morality; it is Christ himself, the eternal Word of God incarnate.

16   Lorenz Cardinal Jaeger, *A Stand on Ecumenism. The Council's Decree* (London: Geoffrey Chapman, 1965), pp. 105-109.

17   Villain, *Vers l'Unité*, p. 40.

18   Flannery, *The Documents of Vatican II*, pp. 483-501.

19   Flannery, *The Documents of Vatican II*, pp. 515-534.

20   Flannery, *The Documents of Vatican II*, p. 491.

Chapter Five

1   The material in this section is largely drawn from "L'abbé Couturier, l'oecuménisme spirituel et la communauté de Grandchamp," in *L'oecuménisme spirituel de Paul Couturier aux défies actuels. Actes du colloque universitaire et interconfessionnel, Lyon et Francheville (Rhône, France), les 8-10 novembre 2002.* Université catholique de Lyon, Faculté de théologie, 77 (Lyon : Éditions PROFAC, 2003).

2   Monod published a pamphlet, outlining his project, inspired by the lifestyle of third order Franciscans: *Le 'tiers ordre' protestant: Les Veilleurs* (Nantes, 10 July 1925).

3   This community of Olivetan Benedictine women, since 1949, lives alongside the Benedictine monks at Bec-Hellouin. The Community of Grandchamp continues to maintain bonds of friendship today with the brothers and sisters of this foundation at Bec, and with related monasteries in Israel and in Ireland.

4   For the history of this dialogue, see Catherine E. Clifford, *The Groupe des Dombes: A Dialogue of Conversion* (New York: Peter Lang, 1995).

5   Geneviève Micheli to Marguerite de Beaumont, February 8, 1940. In "Lettres de Mère Geneviève," (Grandchamp, 1964), p. 68.

6   Genviève Micheli to Marguerite de Beaumont, February 28, 1940. In "Lettres," p. 69.

7   Marguerite de Beaumont, *Du grain à l'épi* (Éditions Ouverture, 1995), p. 187. These words were penned when she was eighty years of age.

8   Ibid.

9   Geneviève Micheli to Marguerite de Beaumont, April 23, 1940. In "Lettres," p. 75.

10   Maurice Villain, *L'abbé Paul Couturier et l'unité chrétienne* (Tournai : Casterman, 1959), p. 192.

11   Paul Couturier to Marguerite de Beaumont, April 3, 1940. In "Lettres," p. 71.

12   Paul Couturier to Marguerite de Beaumont, August 14, 1940. In "Lettres," p. 72.

13   Paul Couturier to Marguerite de Beaumont, September 24, 1940. In "Lettres," p. 72.

14   Paul Couturier to Marguerite de Beaumont, March 3, 1941. In "Lettres," p. 73.

15   Geoffrey Curtis, *Paul Couturier and Unity in Christ* (London: SCM Press, 1964), p. 239.

16   Brother Roger of Taizé, *Parable of Community* (Taizé: Les Presses de Taizé, 1980), p. 13. The most recent edition of the "Rule of Taizé" appears in *The Sources of Taizé* (Chicago: GIA Publications, 2000).

17   A liturgy of the hours, produced through the influence of the movement "Église et Liturgy" was the basis of their daily prayer: *L'Office divin de chaque jour*, 2nd edition (Delachaux et Niestlé, 1953). It later became the basis of the "Office of Taizé," *La lounge des jours* (Taizé: Les Presses de Taizé, 1971); ET: *Praise in All Our Days* (Leighton Buzzard: Faith Press, 1975).

Chapter Six

1   For a critical examination of the historical sources for this emergence of the Baptists and the relationship of the Smyth congregation to the Mennonites, see James Robert Coggins, *John Smyth's Congregation: English Separatism, Mennonite Influence, and the Elect Nation.* Studies in Anabaptist and Mennonite History, 32. (Waterloo, ON: Herald Press, 1991), pp. 61-65. Smyth set forth the theological rationale for his rejection of the baptisms of other churches as "anti-Christian" in his 1609 treatise *The Character of the Beast of the False Constitution of the Church*, in W. T. Whitley, ed., *The Works of John Smyth, Fellow of Christ's College, 1594-8*, 2 vols. (Cambridge: Cambridge University Press, 1915).

2   *Baptism, Eucharist and Ministry*, Faith and Order Paper No. 111 (Geneva: World Council of Churches, 1982). For published Baptist responses, see William R. Estep, "A Response to *Baptism, Eucharist and Ministry*: Faith and Order Paper No. 111," in William H. Brackney and R. J. Burke, eds., *Faith, Life and Witness: The Papers of the Study and Research Division of the Baptist World Alliance 1986-1990* (Birmingham, Ala.: Samford University Press, 1990), pp. 2-16; Max Thurian, ed.,

Churches Respond to Baptism, Eucharist and Ministry, 6 vols. (Geneva: World Council of Churches, 1986-88); and *Baptism, Eucharist and Ministry 1982-1990: Report of the Process and the Responses*, Faith and Order Paper No. 149 (Geneva: World Council of Churches, 1990). A notable positive Baptist response to BEM came from the Myanmar (formerly Burma) Baptist Convention, which not only publicly affirmed the call of BEM to refrain from the rebaptism of those previously baptized as infants but also commended the document to the churches of the Convention to use as a study guide to help Baptists appreciate the theological significance of infant baptism in other communions (reported in Anglican Consultative Council and Baptist World Alliance, *Conversations Around the World 2000-2005: The Report of the International Conversations between the Anglican Communion and the Baptist World Alliance* [London: The Anglican Communion Office, 2005], pp. 50-51).

3   Coggins, *John Smyth's Congregation*, pp. 77-81.

4   According to the most recent edition of the *Handbook of Denominations in the United States*, 12th ed., ed. Frank S. Mead, Samuel S. Hill, and Craig D. Atwood (Nashville, TN: Abingdon Press, 2005), pp. 181-217, there are at least thirty-one national-level Baptist conventions or denomination-like organizations in the United States.

5   Timothy F. George, *Faithful Witness: The Life and Mission of William Carey* (Birmingham, AL: New Hope, 1991), p. 162.

6   By-laws of the Faith and Order Commission of the World Council of Churches, quoted in *Faith and Order: Toward a North American Conference. Study Guide*, ed. Norman A. Hjelm (Grand Rapids, MI: William B. Eerdmans, 2005), p. vii.

7   A series of pamphlets on "Baptist Myths" co-sponsored by the Baptist History and Heritage Society, the Center for Baptist Studies of Mercer University, and the William H. Whitsitt Historical Society included the pamphlet "Myth: Baptists Are Anti-Ecumenical" by Glenn Jonas (Brentwood, TN: Baptist History and Heritage Society, 2003), which called attention to William Carey's 1806 ecumenical proposal, Baptist participation in the formation of the World Council of Churches and the National Council of Churches in the USA, and such notable Baptist advocates of organic church union across denominational lines as British Baptists John H. Shakespeare and Ernest A. Payne. That a pamphlet of this nature needed to be published illustrates the pervasiveness of the perception that Baptists are not the most ecumenically inclined members of the body of Christ, even while supplying evidence to the contrary.

8   H. Leon McBeth, *The Baptist Heritage: Four Centuries of Baptist Witness* (Nashville, TN: Broadman Press, 1987), pp. 86-91.

9   The article on "Last Things" in the *Baptist Faith and Message* adopted by the Southern Baptist Convention in 1963, for example, affirms that "God, in His

own time and in His own way, will bring the world to its appropriate end." See William L. Lumpkin, *Baptist Confessions of Faith*, rev. ed. (Valley Forge, PA: Judson Press, 1969), p. 397. This language is retained in the most recent revision of this confession in 2000.

10   Most of the individuals, institutions, and denominations noted in a section titled "The Rise and Spread of Dispensationalism" in Craig A. Blaising and Darrell L. Bock, *Progressive Dispensationalism* (Grand Rapids, MI: Baker Books, 2000), pp. 10-13, have Baptist and Free Church connections.

11   A confidence that Free Church patterns of ecclesial life represent the ecumenical future is evident in two apologies for Baptist identity from the first decade of the twentieth century: Walter Rauschenbusch, *Why I Am a Baptist* (Philadelphia: Baptist Leader, 1958; originally published as a series of articles in *Rochester Baptist Monthly* vol. 20 [1905-06]), and E. Y. Mullins, *The Axioms of Religion: A New Interpretation of the Baptist Faith* (Philadelphia: American Baptist Publication Society, 1908). By the time Southern Baptist historian William R. Estep published his largely negative book-length assessment of Faith and Order ecumenism in the wake of the New Delhi Assembly and Vatican II, *Baptists and Christian Unity* (Nashville, TN: Broadman Press, 1966), it was manifest that representatives of the Free Church tradition constituted an ecclesiological minority within the Faith and Order movement. This factor has contributed to the widespread conviction that Baptist participation in any form of organic unity would require the surrender of key Baptist ecclesiological distinctives.

12   James Wm. McClendon, Jr., *Systematic Theology*, 3 vols. (Nashville: Abingdon, 1986-2000). An accessible introduction to the aims and distinctive achievements of McClendon's project is provided by Curtis W. Freeman, "A Theology for Brethren, Radical Believers, and Other Baptists," *Brethren Life and Thought* 50, nos. 1-2 (Winter-Spring 2006): 106-15.

13   McClendon, *Systematic Theology*, vol. 2, *Doctrine*, p. 68.

14   McClendon, *Systematic Theology*, vol. 1, *Ethics*, rev. ed., pp. 26-34; see especially p. 30: "Scripture in this vision effects a link between the church of the apostles and our own. So the vision can be expressed as a hermeneutical principle: shared awareness of the present Christian community as the primitive community and the eschatological community. In a motto, the church now is the primitive church and the church on judgment day."

15   McClendon, *Systematic Theology*, vol. 2, *Doctrine*, p. 96; cf. Paul Althaus, *Die Letzen Dinge: Lehrbuch der Eschatologie* (Gütersloh: Gerd Mohr, 1948), p. 29.

16   McClendon, *Systematic Theology*, vol. 2, *Doctrine*, p. 75-89.

17   On the use of this passage in major ecumenical texts associated with dialogue between the Roman Catholic Church and other ecclesial bodies, see Hellen

Mardaga, "Reflection on the Meaning of John 17:21 for Ecumenical Dialogue," *Ecumenical Trends* 34, no. 10 (November 2005): 148-52.

18   Cf. Oscar Cullmann, *Christ and Time: The Primitive Christian Conception of Time and History*, trans. F. V. Filson (London: SCM Press, 1950).

19   When Baptists have affirmed catholicity as a mark of the church, they have tended to understand catholicity in terms of the church's invisible or "mystical" oneness. The *Orthodox Creed*, a confession adopted by a group of English General Baptist congregations in 1678, exemplifies this understanding in article 30: "[W]e believe the visible church of Christ on earth, is made up of several distinct congregations, which make up that one catholick church, or mystical body of Christ" (Lumpkin, *Baptist Confessions of Faith*, pp. 318-19).

20   World Council of Churches, *The New Delhi Report: The Third Assembly of the World Council of Churches 1961*, ed. Willem A. Visser't Hooft (London: SCM Press, 1962), p. 116.

21   Nigel G. Wright, *Disavowing Constantine: Mission, Church and the Social Order in the Theologies of John Howard Yoder and Jürgen Moltmann* (Carlisle: Paternoster, 2000); *Free Church, Free State: The Positive Baptist Vision* (Milton Keynes: Paternoster, 2005), especially pp. 204-50.

22   Second Vatican Council, Declaration on Religious Liberty (*Dignitatis Humanae*), (7 December 1965), in *Vatican Council II: The Conciliar and Post Conciliar Documents*, rev. ed., ed. Austin Flannery (Northport, NY: Costello, 1992), pp. 799-812. Karl Barth, however, detected a hint of vestigial Constantinianism even in this declaration, as reflected in the critical question raised in *Ad Limina Apostolorum: An Appraisal of Vatican II*, trans. Keith R. Crim (Richmond, VA: John Knox Press, 1968). p. 40: "When or where did the witnesses in the Old and New Testaments demand a legally assured scope for their life and the proclamation of their faith, and for the presentation of other religions?" It must be conceded that the same critical question could also be addressed to Baptist arguments for the constitutional separation of church and state in the United States.

23   Wright, *Free Church, Free State*, pp. xviii-xx.

24   Vincent of Lérins *Commonitorium* 2.1-3, in G. Rauschen and P. B. Albers, eds., *Florilegium Patristicum*, vol. 5, *Vincentii Lerinensis Commonitoria*, ed. G. Rauschen (Bonn: P. Hanstein, 1906), p. 12; ET in *Nicene and Post-Nicene Fathers*, Second Series, ed. Philip Schaff and Henry Wace (New York: Christian Literature Publishing Co., 1887-94; reprint, Peabody, Mass.: Hendrickson Publishers, 1994), vol. 11, p. 132. This insistence on the consent of the faithful might also be construed as a radical extension to the whole communion of saints of the Conciliar Movement by means of which the church reformed itself prior to and in the wake of the Protestant Reformation. On this now-neglected tradition of

ecclesial authority, see Paul Avis, *Beyond the Reformation? Authority, Primacy and Unity in the Conciliar Tradition* (London: T&T Clark, 2006).

25   On the possibility that the dissent of the Free Churches has in fact made positive contributions to the quest for unity, see James Wm. McClendon, Jr. and John Howard Yoder, "Christian Unity in Ecumenical Perspective: A Response to David Wayne Layman," *Journal of Ecumenical Studies* 27, no. 3 (Summer 1990): 561-80 (see especially the subsection "How Free Churches Have Made for Unity," pp. 576-78).

26   *Catechism of the Catholic Church* (Liguori, MO: Liguori Publications, 1994), no. 1546, p. 386: "Christ, high priest and unique mediator, has made of the church 'a kingdom, priests for his God and Father.' The whole community of believers is, as such, priestly. The faithful exercise their baptismal priesthood through their participation, each according to his own vocation, in Christ's mission as priest, prophet, and king."

27   In addition to the annual Week of Prayer for Christian Unity, following the Ecumenical Prayer Cycle during prayers of intercession in weekly corporate worship provides congregations with a regular opportunity to participate in the unifying practice of prayer for sisters and brothers in Christ who are members of other churches.

28   Visser't Hooft, ed., *The New Delhi Report*, p. 116.

29   Robert W. Jenson, "God's Time, Our Time: An Interview with Robert W. Jenson," *Christian Century* 123/9 (May 2, 2006): 31-35, offered this candid assessment of the reasons for the failure of the proposed conference: "It was undone by mainline Protestantism's present indifference to and distraction from the whole matter, by evangelicalism's unconcern about separation at the Lord's table, and by deliberate obstruction from within the established ecumenical apparatus" (p. 33).

30   Congregation for the Doctrine of the Faith, "Responses to Some Questions Regarding Certain Aspects of the Doctrine on the Church [10 July 2007]," *Origins* 37, no. 9 (July 19, 2007): 134-136.

31   Second Vatican Council, Decree on Ecumenism (*Unitatis Redintegratio*), (21 November 1964), in *Vatican Council II*, ed. Flannery, pp. 452-73; John Paul II, *Ut Unum Sint: Encyclical Letter of the Holy Father John Paul II on Commitment to Ecumenism* (Boston: Pauline Books and Media, 1995).

Contributors

CATHERINE E. CLIFFORD is Associate Professor of Systematic and Historical Theology in the Faculty of Theology, Saint Paul University, in Ottawa, Canada. The author of *The Groupe des Dombes: A Dialogue of Conversion* (New York: Peter Lang, 2005), she is President is of the International Network of Societies of Catholic Theology, and has served for many years as a member of the Anglican Roman Catholic Dialogue Commission in Canada.

STEVEN R. HARMON is Associate Professor of Divinity at Beeson Divinity School, Samford University, Birmingham, Alabama, USA, and previously served on the faculty of Campbell University Divinity School in Buies Creek, North Carolina, USA. The author of *Towards Baptist Catholicity: Essays on Tradition and the Baptist Vision* (Paternoster, 2006), he is Vice Chair of the Doctrine and Interchurch Cooperation Commission of the Baptist World Alliance, a member of the Baptist World Alliance delegation to a five-year series of theological conversations with the Pontifical Council for Promoting Christian Unity currently underway, and a member of the Faith and Order Commission of the National Council of Churches of Christ, USA.

WALTER CARDINAL KASPER is an accomplished theologian, having taught dogmatic theology at the Universities of Münster and Tübingen, and lectured as Visiting Professor at the Catholic University of America in Washington, D.C. In 1989 he was ordained Bishop of the Diocese of Rottenburg-Stuttgart, Germany, and since 2001 has served as the President of the Pontifical Council for the Promotion of Christian Unity. He has published many scholarly articles and books, including two recent titles devoted to work and prayer for the unity of Christians, *That They May All be*

One (London: Burns and Oates, 2004) and *A Handbook of Spiritual Ecumenism* (New York: New City, 2007).

JAMES F. PUGLISI holds a chair in Ecumenics at the Pontifical Athenaeum "Antonianum," Rome, and lectures in ecumenical theology at the Pontifical University of Saint Thomas Aquinas, Rome. He is the author of the three volume study, *The Process of Admission to Ordained Ministry: A Comparative Study* (Collegeville, Liturgical Press, 1996), and is the editor of two volumes of collected essays, *Liturgical Renewal as a Way to Christian Unity* (Collegeville: Liturgical Press, 2005), and *Petrine Ministry and the Unity of the Church* (Collegeville: Liturgical Press, 1999). He is Director of the Centro Pro Unione in Rome, and Minister General of the Franciscan Friars of the Atonement.

CHARLES SHERLOCK has taught Systematic and Liturgical Theology at Trinity and Ridley Colleges, Melbourne, Australia. He is the author of *The Doctrine of Humanity* (InterVaristy Press, 1996) and the editor of *A Pastoral Handbook for Anglicans* (Melbourne: Acorn Press, 2001). From 2003-2007 he served as the Director of Ministry Studies Melbourne College of Divinity, and now works in theological education for the Anglican diocese of Bendigo. He is Executive Secretary of the Liturgical Commission of the Anglican Church in Australia and has been a member of the Anglican Roman Catholic International Commission since 1991.

GEORGE H. TAVARD (†2007) taught theology at Assumption College, Worchester, MA, Mount Mercy College (Carlow University), Pittsburgh, and Methodist Theological School, Ohio. He authored over forty books in English and French, including *Vatican II and the Ecumenical Way* (Milwaukee: Marquette University Press, 2006), *The Starting Point of Calvin's Theology* (Grand Rapids: Eerdmans, 2000), and *The Church, Community of Salvation* (Collegeville: Liturgical Press, 1991). He served as a member of the Anglican Roman Catholic International Commission (1968-

1983), the International Dialogue of the Roman Catholic Church and the World Methodist Council (1983-2005), and took part in the Anglican Roman Catholic and Lutheran Roman Catholic dialogues in the United States. He was a recipient of the John Courtney Murray Award accorded by the Catholic Theological Society of America for his contribution to theology.

SISTER MINKE DE VRIES is the former prioress of the Community of Grandchamp (1970-1999), near Neuchatel, Switzerland. She is the author of *Vers une gratuité féconde* (Éditions Paulines, 2008).